GOD OF A HU

GOD
OF A HUNDRED
NAMES

*PRAYERS OF MANY PEOPLES
AND CREEDS*

collected and arranged

by

BARBARA GREENE

and

VICTOR GOLLANCZ

HODDER AND STOUGHTON
LONDON   SYDNEY   AUCKLAND   TORONTO

God is hidden, no man knoweth his form,
No man has searched out his similitude.
He is hidden to gods and men. He is a secret to all his
    creatures.
No man knoweth a name by which to call him.
His name is hidden. His name is a secret to all his children.
His names are without number.
His names are many; no man knoweth the number thereof.

OLD EGYPTIAN

In that day shall the Lord be one, and his name one.

HEBREW

PREFACE

Many years ago I planned a ludicrously ambitious project. My idea was to get together, from all available sources and with the aid of many specialists and translators, a great collection of such prayers, in the widest sense of the word, as had survived, not only in the literature, but also in the oral tradition, of every religion, "lower" as well as "higher", that had anywhere, and at any period of history, expressed the hopes, the fears and the spiritual aspirations of mankind. The result, I hoped, would be a vast body of material, which could then be organized into a volume of manageable proportions: and though I promised myself to be as objectively scientific as possible, I believed that certain conclusions would follow which would greatly delight me.

So overweening an ambition—and a lifetime, anyhow, would have been required to implement it—of course came to nothing: and I mention it only for the purpose of indicating, by way of contrast, the origin and nature of the present collection—which are as follows:

A few weeks ago Barbara Greene, who was then, to my loss, unknown to me, sent my firm a collection of prayers. She wrote that, in view of my [spasmodic] internationalist and anti-particularist activities, she thought they might interest me personally: and she added a line or two about her method and purpose.

She had long been interested, she explained, in a certain unity observable behind and beyond the apparently most disparate creeds; and she had formed the habit of jotting down, over a period of years, any prayers she might happen upon such as illustrated this theme, together with others—and these were the more numerous—that specially appealed to her by reason of some particular interest or beauty. The collection she was sending us was the result.

I took the manuscript home immediately, and read it with delight. She and I are of different confessions, if indeed "confession" has any meaning in my case: she is a Roman Catholic, and a practising one, while I am nothing in particular (when driven into a corner I sometimes describe myself as a liberal, non-practising Judaeo-Christian). But I at once recognized in her, if she will allow me to say so, a music that harmonized with my own: and as I also had assembled a collection, with motives rather similar to hers, I ventured to suggest that she might be willing to accept me as a collaborator. I would add my collection to hers; would supply notes; and, as I like arranging things (to excess, my critics might say), would charge myself with the job of classification. She graciously agreed, and the present volume is the outcome.

It will at once be apparent from the above what the book emphatically is not. It is not a study in comparative religion, on however modest a scale: there is nothing scientific about it: no research, even of the briefest or sketchiest kind, has gone into its making. An accidental sort of book—that perhaps is the way to describe it. Here was material we had casually assembled for our own pleasure; and hoping that others might take pleasure in it too, we decided to publish.

Primarily, then, we offer our collection as a small treasury of spiritual refreshment: and if any, whatever their religion or formal lack of it (in the ordinary sense), should find here a useful source-book for prayer or meditation, particularly before and after sleep, we should be happy. But we have a secondary motive too, as will already be clear: and we are anxious that it should not be misunderstood.

We have by no means sought to prove that, essentially at any rate, no difference exists between any one religion—or even between any one monotheistic religion—and any other: this is not an essay in what Catholics call "indifferentism".

Nor would we deny for a moment that anyone could put a volume together with a tendency other than, indeed opposite to, that of ours. We might, for instance, have juxtaposed prayers to the merciful Father of all His creatures with what are also called prayers, and can alas readily enough be found, to a particularist god of vengeance for the eternal damnation of "his" enemies: or we might have contrasted petitions for personal advantage (we have in fact included a very few of these, for their great beauty) with varying expressions of the quintessential "Thy will be done". Such a procedure, if implemented with sufficient knowledge, might have interested students of comparative religion: but it would not have interested us.

Our hope is altogether more modest: namely, that by bringing together a number of prayers that we have happened upon we may have illustrated, haphazardly enough, a by no means unfamiliar theme. Which is this:

From amidst diversified and often warring creeds: over a vast span of history: in the language of many a tribe and many a nation: out of the mouths of the learned and simple, the lowly and great: despite oceans of bloodshed, and torturing inhumanities, and persecutions unspeakable—the single voice of a greater Humanity rises confidently to heaven, saying "We adore Thee, who art One and who art Love: and it is in unity and love that we would live together, doing Thy will".

If those who have heard this voice in their own hearts would be resolutely true to it in their thinking about races and nations other than their own—and about those, more especially, who think it a snare and a delusion—then indeed would our darkness be lightened, and the world's poisoned water be turned into wine.

We have prefaced each of our sections with a meditation, and have also included a "prayer" or two in which God is the speaker: believing, with John Saltmarsh, that "Prayer is no

9

other but the revelation of the will or mind of God", and with Rabbi Pinhas of Korez that "The people think that they pray before God. But it is not so. For the prayer itself is the essence of the Godhead". We have also occasionally printed the Hebrew, Latin, French or German original, with a translation. There has been no system about this: we have simply followed our whim.

When the author of a prayer or meditation first appears, his dates are given (unless it would be otiose to do so): but not subsequently.

Notes on a number of religions, and a few other notes, will be found at the end of the book. The remainder are printed, in smaller type, with the prayers.

While I have been happily arranging and re-arranging the prayers here in Florence, two of my colleagues have been co-operating with me in London. My daughter Livia has been dealing with the rather complicated typography, and my friend James MacGibbon has been checking texts and references and helping me with the notes. I am very grateful to them both. I am also grateful to The Garden City Press of Letchworth for the devoted care they have shown throughout.

V.G.

The Green Cloister, Florence
April 30th, 1962

FOREWORD

Prayer is a road to spiritual knowledge. The nations refuse to share their scientific knowledge, and are being brought by their intransigence to the very brink of international disaster. One hope remains: namely that more and more groupings may seek to find a basis for unity in the spiritual dimension. Several efforts in this direction had already been made, when in January 1962 a remarkable meeting took place in Rome under the Presidency of Cardinal Bea, who had been appointed head of the Secretariat of Christian Unity by Pope John XXIII. The representatives included Catholics, Orthodox, Jews, and Moslems, and those of several other creeds. The proceedings opened with a Mass according to the Maronite rite. In the course of his welcoming speech the Cardinal said that those present were united by a deep faith in one sole God, the creator of the universe, ruler of all nations and father of all mankind. "Perhaps few among you," he said, "have so many dealings with men of different races, different religions, different beliefs and different cultures as I—unworthily—have. In all these dealings I have always found that a great love, a wide-open heart, always opens the hearts of others. This great love must be not mere diplomacy but the result of an inner conviction that, as I have already said, we are all children of one God, who has created mankind, who has created each one of us, and whose children we all are."

May this book of prayers help towards a deeper understanding.

It would be quite impossible for me to name all those friends from all over the world who have sent me prayers and who have helped me in bringing together my collection, but I would particularly like to thank my mother for her great interest throughout the years, my friends Mrs. Margaret Kiskadden of California, Baroness Elizabeth von Bültzings- lôwen of Liechtenstein, Mrs. Olga Collett, and my cousin Christopher Isherwood, who was so encouraging when I began my collection many years ago.

B.G.

CONTENTS

NOTE

The music on page 213 is part of the *Heiliger Dankgesang*
from Beethoven's Quartet in A minor, opus 132: a prayer
of thanksgiving for his recovery.

FIRST PART

I. MORNING PRAYER

MEDITATION

Say to thyself, Marcus, at dawn: today I shall run up against the busy-body, the ungrateful, the overbearing, the deceitful, the envious, the self-centred. All this has fallen to their lot because they are ignorant of good and evil. But I, understanding the nature of the Good, that it is fair, and of Evil, that it is ugly, and the nature of the evil-doer himself, that he is my kin—as sharing, not indeed the same blood and seed, but intelligence and a spark of the Divine—can neither be damaged by any of them (for no one can involve me in what is disgraceful) nor can be angry with my kinsman or estranged from him. For we have been born for cooperation, as have feet, hands, eyelids and the rows of upper and lower teeth. Therefore to thwart one another is unnatural; and we do thwart one another when we shew resentment and dislike.

MARCUS AURELIUS · ROMAN EMPEROR · STOIC

We bless Thee for our creation.

THE BOOK OF COMMON PRAYER

O my God, the soul which thou gavest me is pure.

THE HEBREW MORNING SERVICE

Blessed art thou, O Lord our God, King of the universe, who hast given to the cock intelligence to distinguish between day and night.

THE HEBREW MORNING SERVICE

Blessed art thou, O Lord our God, King of the universe, who createst thy world every morning afresh.

HEBREW · CONTEMPORARY

Is not sight a jewel? Is not hearing a treasure? Is not speech a glory? O my Lord pardon my ingratitude, and pity my dullness who am not sensible of these gifts. The freedom of thy bounty hath deceived me. These things were too near to be considered. Thou presentedst me with Thy blessings, and I was not aware. But now I give thanks and adore and praise Thee for Thine inestimable favors.

THOMAS TRAHERNE · 1637?–74

TO CHRIST OUR LORD

Hail, heavenly beam, brightest of angels thou,
sent unto men upon this middle-earth!
Thou art the true refulgence of the sun,

radiant above the stars, and from thyself
illuminest for ever all the tides of time.
And as thou, God indeed begotten of God,
thou Son of the true Father, wast from aye,
without beginning, in the heaven's glory,
so now thy handiwork in its sore need
prayeth thee boldly that thou send to us
the radiant sun, and that thou come thyself
to enlighten those who for so long a time
were wrapt around with darkness, and here in
     gloom
have sat the livelong night, shrouded in sin.

CYNEWULF · ANGLO-SAXON · 8TH CENTURY

The translation is by Sir Israel Gollancz.

These words of glory of the God who is light shall be
words supreme amongst things that are great. I glorify Varuna
almighty, the God who is loving towards him who adores.

We praise thee with our thoughts, O God. We praise thee
even as the sun praises thee in the morning: may we find joy
in being thy servants.

Keep us under thy protection. Forgive our sins and give
us thy love.

God made the rivers to flow. They feel no weariness,
they cease not from flowing. They fly swiftly like birds in
the air.

May the stream of my life flow into the river of righteousness. Loose the bonds of sin that bind me. Let not the
thread of my song be cut while I sing; and let not my work
end before its fulfilment.

Remove all fear from me, O Lord. Receive me graciously
unto thee, O king. Cut off the bonds of afflictions that bind
me: I cannot even open mine eyes without thy help . . .

We will sing thy praises, O God almighty. We will now

and evermore sing thy praises, even as they were sung of old.
For thy laws are immutable, O God: they are firm like the
mountains.

Forgive the trespasses that I may have committed. Many
mornings remain to dawn upon us: lead us through them all,
O God.

RIG-VEDA · HINDU

The translation is by Juan Mascaró. And see note on
page 281.

Thanks to Thee, O God, that I have risen today,
    To the rising of this life itself;
May it be to Thine own glory, O God of every gift,
    And to the glory of my soul likewise.

O great God, aid Thou my soul
    With the aiding of Thine own mercy;
Even as I clothe my body with wool,
    Cover Thou my soul with the shadow of Thy wing;

Help me to avoid every sin,
    And the source of every sin to forsake;
And as the mist scatters on the crest of the hills,
    May each ill haze clear from my soul, O God.

GAELIC

The translation is by Alexander Carmichael, as is that of
all the Gaelic prayers in this book. And see note on page
287.

O God, who broughtst me from the rest of last night
Unto the joyous light of this day,
Be Thou bringing me from the new light of this day

Unto the guiding light of eternity.
Oh! from the new light of this day
Unto the guiding light of eternity.

GAELIC

O Heavenly Father . . . I most heartily thank Thee, that it hath pleased Thy fatherly goodness to take care of me this night past. I most entirely beseech Thee, O most merciful Father, to show the like kindness toward me this day, in preserving my body and soul; that I may neither think, breathe, speak, nor do anything that may be displeasing to Thy fatherly goodness, dangerous to myself, or hurtful to my neighbour; but that all my doings may be agreeable to Thy most blessed will, which is always good; that they may advance Thy glory, answer to my vocation, and profit my neighbour, whom I ought to love as myself; that, whensoever Thou callest me hence, I may be found the child not of darkness but of light; through Jesus Christ our Lord, Amen.

THOMAS BECON · 1512–67

Thomas Becon was chaplain to Archbishop Cranmer.

O Lord our God, Who hast bidden the light to shine out of darkness, Who hast again awakened us to praise Thy goodness and ask for Thy grace: accept now, in Thy endless mercy, the sacrifice of our worship and thanksgiving, and grant unto us all such requests as may be wholesome for us. Make us to be children of the light and of the day, and heirs of Thy everlasting inheritance. Remember, O Lord, according to the multitude of Thy mercies, Thy whole Church: all who join with us in prayer; all our brethren by land or sea, or wherever they may be in Thy vast Kingdom, who stand in need of Thy grace and succour. Pour out upon them the riches of Thy mercy, so that we, redeemed in soul and body,

and steadfast in faith, may ever praise Thy wonderful and
holy name. Amen.

EASTERN CHURCH

Praised be Thou, O God, Almighty Ruler, Who dost make
the day bright with Thy sunshine, and the night with the
beams of heavenly fires!

Listen now to our prayers, and forgive us both our
conscious and unconscious transgressions.

Clothe us with the armour of righteousness; shield us with
Thy truth; watch over us with Thy power; save us from all
calamity; and give us grace to pass all the days of our life
blameless, holy, peaceful, free from sin, terror and offence.
For with Thee is mercy and plenteous redemption, our Lord
and God, and to Thee we bring our thanks and praise. Amen.

EASTERN CHURCH

Into the hands of Thy blessed protection and unspeakable
mercy, O Lord, I commend this day my soul and my body,
with all the faculties, powers and actions of them both;
beseeching Thee to be ever with me, to direct, sanctify, and
govern me in the ways of Thy laws, and in the works of Thy
commandments; that, through Thy most mighty protection,
both here and ever, I may be preserved in body and soul,
to serve Thee, the only true God, through Jesus Christ our
Lord. Amen.

ANONYMOUS · 16TH CENTURY

O Lord, support us all the day long of this troublous life,
until the shadows lengthen and the evening comes, and the
busy world is hushed, and the fever of life is over, and our

work is done. Then, Lord, in Thy mercy, grant us a safe lodging, a holy rest, and peace at the last.

ANONYMOUS · PROBABLY 16TH CENTURY

This was a favourite prayer of Cardinal Newman.

Help us this day, O God, to serve Thee devoutly, and the world busily. May we do our work wisely, give succour secretly, go to meat appetitely, sit thereat discreetly, arise temperately, please our friend duly, go to bed merrily, and sleep surely; for the joy of our Lord, Jesus Christ, Amen.

TRADITIONAL · MIDDLE AGES

O Lord, grant me to greet the coming day in peace. Help me in all things to rely upon Thy holy will. Bless my dealings with all who surround me. Teach me to treat all that comes to me throughout the day with peace of soul, and with firm conviction that Thy will governs all. Teach me to act firmly and wisely, without embittering and embarrassing others. Give me strength to bear the fatigue of the coming day with all that it shall bring. Teach me to pray.

THE METROPOLITAN PHILARET OF MOSCOW

He compiled a great catechism of the Eastern Church for the use of Russian clergy and schoolmasters in giving religious instruction. When Dean Stanley met him in Moscow in the 1850's he said "Never have I seen such respect shown to any Ecclesiastic".

Grant that, this day and every day, we may keep our shock of wonder at each new beauty that comes upon us as we walk down the paths of life: and that we may say in our hearts, when horror and ugliness intervene, Thy will be done.

ANONYMOUS · CONTEMPORARY

FIRST PART

II. FOR THE DAY'S WORK

MEDITATION

The worst of partialities is to withhold oneself, the worst ignorance is not to act, the worst lie is to steal away.

CHARLES PÉGUY · 1873–1914

1

O Lord, let us not live to be useless, for Christ's sake.

JOHN WESLEY · 1703–91

Thou, O God, dost sell us all good things at the price of labour.

LEONARDO DA VINCI

These things, good Lord, that we pray for, give us Thy grace to labour for.

SIR THOMAS MORE · 1478–1535

Teach us, good Lord, to serve Thee as Thou deservest; to give and not count the cost, to fight and not heed the wounds, to toil and not seek for rest, to labour and not ask for any reward, save that of knowing that we do Thy will.

ST. IGNATIUS LOYOLA · 1491–1556 · ADAPTATION

Ignatius Loyola was the founder of the Society of Jesus (Jesuits).

God give me work
Till my life shall end
And life
Till my work is done.

WINIFRED HOLTBY · 1898–1935

Written on the novelist's grave at Rudstone, Yorkshire.

O Lord, Thou knowest how busy I must be this day. If I forget Thee, do not forget me.

JACOB ASTLEY · 1579–1652

His battle-prayer at Edgehill.

O Lord God, when Thou givest to Thy servants to endeavour any great matter, grant us to know that it is not the beginning but the continuing of the same, until it be thoroughly finished, which yieldeth the true glory.

SIR FRANCIS DRAKE · c.1545–96

Written on the day he sailed into Cadiz.

O God, Who hast commanded that no man should be idle, give us grace to employ all our talents and faculties in the service appointed for us; that, whatsoever our hand findeth to do, we may do it with our might.

JAMES MARTINEAU · PHILOSOPHER · 1805–1900

I thank Thee, my Creator and Lord, that Thou hast given me these joys in Thy creation, this ecstasy over the works of Thy hands. I have made known the glory of Thy works to men as far as my finite spirit was able to comprehend Thy infinity. If I have said anything wholly unworthy of Thee, or have aspired after my own glory, graciously forgive me. Amen.

JOHANN KEPLER · ASTRONOMER · 1571–1630

His hands were crippled and his eyesight permanently impaired by smallpox at the age of four. He may be called the founder of physical astronomy.

Make us, O Lord, to flourish like pure lilies in the courts of
Thine house, and to show forth to the faithful the fragrance
of good works, and the example of a godly life, through Thy
mercy and grace. Amen.

THE MOZARABIC LITURGY

This was the national liturgy of the Spanish Church till
the end of the eleventh century, when it was superseded
by the Roman liturgy. Its use lingered on for five hundred
years, and in the sixteenth century Cardinal Ximenes
founded a college of priests at Toledo to perpetuate its
use. It still survives there.

O God, who hast ordained that whatever is to be desired,
should be sought by labour, and who, by thy blessing,
bringest honest labour to good effect; look with mercy upon
my studies and endeavours. Grant me, O Lord, to design
only what is lawful and right; and afford me calmness of
mind, and steadiness of purpose, that I may so do thy will in
this short life, as to obtain happiness in the world to come,
for the sake of Jesus Christ our Lord. Amen.

SAMUEL JOHNSON · 1709–84

O heavenly Father, the Father of all wisdom, understanding, and true strength, I beseech Thee look mercifully
upon me, and send Thy Holy Spirit into my breast; that,
when I must join to fight in the field for the glory of Thy
Holy Name, then I, being strengthened with the defence of
Thy right hand, may manfully stand in the confession of Thy
faith and of Thy truth, and continue in the same unto the
end of my life, through our Lord Jesus Christ. Amen.

NICHOLAS RIDLEY · C.1500–55

Bishop Ridley signed the letters patent settling the
English crown on Lady Jane Grey, and when her

cause was lost was arrested by order of Queen Mary. He refused to recant, and was burnt at the stake as a heretic at Oxford.

Oh, send Thy light and Thy truth, that I may live always near to Thee, my God. Oh, let me feel Thy love, that I may be, as it were, already in heaven, that I may do all my work as the angels do theirs; and oh, let me be ready for every work! be ready to go out or go in, to stay or depart, just as Thou shalt appoint. Lord, let me have no will of my own; or consider my true happiness as depending in the smallest degree on anything that can befall me outwardly, but as consisting altogether in conformity to Thy will. Amen.

HENRY MARTYN · 1781–1812

Henry Martyn, an English missionary to India, translated the whole of the New Testament into Hindustani and Persian. Journeying to Arabia for the purpose of composing an Arabic version, he reached Shiraz, and soon plunged into controversy with disputants of other faiths. The following year, after further exhausting journeys, he died at plague-ridden Tokat in Asia Minor.

THE JOY OF WORK

O giver of thyself! at the vision of thee as joy let our souls flame up to thee as the fire, flow on to thee as the river, permeate thy being as the fragrance of the flower. Give us strength to love, to love fully, our life in its joys and sorrows, in its gains and losses, in its rise and fall. Let us have strength enough fully to see and hear thy universe and to work with full vigour therein. Let us fully live the life thou hast given us, let us bravely take and bravely give. This is our prayer to thee. Let us once for all dislodge from our minds the feeble fancy that would make out thy joy to be a thing apart from action, thin, formless, and unsustained. Wherever the peasant tills the hard earth, there does thy joy gush out in the green of the corn, wherever man displaces the entangled forest, smooths the stony ground, and clears for himself a homestead, there does thy joy enfold it in orderliness and peace.

O worker of the universe! We would pray to thee to let the irresistible current of thy universal energy come like the impetuous south wind of spring, let it come rushing over the vast field of the life of man, let it bring the scent of many flowers, the murmurings of many woodlands, let it make sweet and vocal the lifelessness of our dried-up soul-life. Let our newly awakened powers cry for unlimited fulfilment in leaf and flower and fruit.

RABINDRANATH TAGORE · 1861–1941

THE DEED

Lord, not for light in darkness do we pray,
Not that the veil be lifted from our eyes,
Nor that the slow ascension of our day
    Be otherwise.

Not for a clearer vision of the things
Whereof the fashioning shall make us great,
Not for remission of the peril and stings
    Of time and fate.

Not for a fuller knowledge of the end
Whereto we travel, bruised yet unafraid,
Nor that the little healing that we lend
    Shall be repaid.

Not these, O Lord. We would not break the bars
Thy wisdom sets about us; we shall climb
Unfetter'd to the secrets of the stars
    In Thy good time.

We do not crave the high perception swift
When to refrain were well, and when fulfil,
Nor yet the understanding strong to sift
    The good from ill.

Not these, O Lord. For these Thou hast reveal'd,
We know the golden season when to reap
The heavy-fruited treasure of the field,
    The hour to sleep.

Not these. We know the hemlock from the rose,
The pure from stain'd, the noble from the base,
The tranquil holy light of truth that glows
    On Pity's face.

We know the paths wherein our feet should press,
Across our hearts are written Thy decrees:
Yet now, O Lord, be merciful to bless
    With more than these.

Grant us the will to fashion as we feel,
Grant us the strength to labour as we know,
Grant us the purpose, ribb'd and edged with steel,
    To strike the blow.

Knowledge we ask not—knowledge Thou hast lent,
But, Lord, the will—there lies our bitter need,
Give us to build above the deep intent
    The deed, the deed.

                JOHN DRINKWATER · 1882–1937

§ 2

"SLOW AND SLEEPY

Loërd, thou clepedest[1] me
and I not ne answerëd thee
But wordës slow and sleepy:
"Thole[2] yiet! Thole a little!"
But "yiet" and "yiet" was endëless,
and "thole a little" a long way is.

ANONYMOUS · 14TH CENTURY

[1] clepedest = calledst.   [2] thole = be patient.

FIRST PART

III. FOR OURSELVES

MEDITATION

Live unto the Dignity of thy Nature, and leave it not disputable at last, whether thou hast been a Man.

SIR THOMAS BROWNE · 1605–82

If none can 'scape Death's dreadfull darte,
  If rich and poor his becke obey,
If strong, if wise, if all do smarte,
  Then I to 'scape shall have no way.
    O grant me grace, O God! that I
    My life may mend, sith I must die!

ROBERT SOUTHWELL · ?1561–95 · JESUIT

During the reign of Queen Elizabeth, Southwell went
from one Catholic family to another secretly administer-
ing the rites of his church. He was finally arrested and
tortured. After three years in prison he was hanged at
Tyburn.

§ 1

Lord, make me an instrument of Thy peace. Where there
is hatred, let me sow love. Where there is injury, pardon.
Where there is doubt, faith. Where there is despair, hope.
Where there is darkness, light. Where there is sadness, joy.
O Divine Master, grant that I may not so much seek to be
consoled as to console; to be understood, as to understand;
to be loved, as to love; for it is in giving that we receive, it
is in pardoning that we are pardoned, and it is in dying that
we are born to Eternal Life.

ST. FRANCIS OF ASSISI

May obedience conquer disobedience within this house,
and may peace triumph over discord here, and generous
giving over avarice, reverence over contempt, speech with
truthful words over lying utterance; may the righteous order
gain the victory over the demon of the lie.

THE YASNA · ZOROASTRIAN

See note on page 286.

O God, make us children of quietness, and heirs of peace.

ST. CLEMENT

St. Clement comes third or fourth in the lists of Bishops of
Rome. He flourished about A.D. 96.

O Lord Jesus Christ, give us a measure of Thy spirit that
we may be enabled to obey Thy teaching to pacify anger, to
take part in pity, to moderate desire, to increase love, to put
away sorrow, to cast away vain-glory, not to be vindictive,
not to fear death, ever entrusting our spirit to immortal God,
who with Thee and the Holy Ghost liveth and reigneth world
without end.

ST. APOLLONIUS

Apollonius, "one of the faithful at that day", was
tried (c. 185) before Perennis for professing Christianity, would not recant, and was beheaded. This prayer
is adapted from part of his defence.

Bestow on me, O Lord, a genial spirit and unwearied
forbearance; a mild, loving, patient heart; kindly looks,
pleasant, cordial speech and manners in the intercourse of
daily life; that I may give offence to none, but as much as in
me lies live in charity with all men. Amen.

JOHANN ARNDT · GERMAN LUTHERAN · 1555–1621

O Lord, baptize our hearts into a sense of the conditions
and need of all men.

GEORGE FOX

George Fox, 1624–1691, was the founder of the Society
of Friends (Quakers).

O God, help us not to despise or oppose what we do not understand.

WILLIAM PENN · QUAKER · 1644–1718

O God, who has revealed to us that of all the virtues Love may for us most clearly describe Thy infinite nature, and that when we selflessly love we approach most nearly to Thy presence: Grant to us therefore this the supreme virtue; for Thou hast shown us that, without it, persistence hardens into pride, peace chills to cold-heartedness and even humility sinks to despair. But enkindled by loving kindness all these virtues become alive, bearing us up into Thy presence where alone our hearts may rest.

GERALD HEARD · CONTEMPORARY

I confess I can see, but I cannot moderate, nor love as I ought. I pray Thee for Thy loving kindness sake supply my want in this particular. And so make me to love all, that I may be a blessing to all: and well pleasing to Thee in all. Teach me wisdom, how to expend my blood, estate, life, and time in Thy service for the good of all, and make all them that are round about me wise and holy as Thou art. That we might all be knit together in Godly Love, and united in Thy service to Thy Honor and Glory.

THOMAS TRAHERNE

Do Thou in me make peace, O light-bringer.

A MANICHAEAN PRAYER

See note on page 283.

O send out thy light and thy truth . . .

FROM PSALM 43

From the unreal lead me to the real.
From darkness lead me to light.
From death lead me to immortality.

THE UPANISHADS · HINDU

See note on page 281.

§ 2

Let us avoid the proud speaking of the Pharisee and learn
humility from the sighs of the Publican as we cry to our
Saviour: Be merciful, Thou who alone art ready to absolve
us.

EASTERN CHURCH

O Lord, put no trust in me; for I shall surely fail if Thou
uphold me not.

ST. FILIPPO DE NERI · 1515–95

O Saviour, pour upon me thy Spirit of meekness and love,
Annihilate the Selfhood in me, be thou all my life,
Guide thou my hand which trembles exceedingly upon the
    rock of ages.

BLAKE

Moonless darkness stands between.
Past, O Past, no more be seen!
But the Bethlehem star may lead me
To the sight of Him who freed me
From the self that I have been.
Make me pure, Lord: Thou art holy:
Make me meek, Lord: Thou wert lowly:

Now beginning, and alway:
Now begin, on Christmas day.

GERARD MANLEY HOPKINS · 1844–89

This is a fragment.

Let the remembrance of all the glory wherein I was created
make me more serious and humble, more deep and penitent,
more pure and holy before Thee.

THOMAS TRAHERNE

O Christ my Lord which for my sinnes
  didst hange upon a tree;
Graunt that thy grace in me, poore wretch,
  may still ingraffed bee.

Graunt that thy naked hanging then
  may kill in me all pride
And care of wealth, sith thou didst there
  in such poor state abide.

Graunt y^t thy crown of pricking thornes,
  which thou for me didst were,
May make me willing for thy sake
  all shame and payne to bare.

Graunt y^t the skornes and tauntes, which thou
  didst on the cross endure,
May humble me, and in my hart
  all pacience still procure.

Graunt that thy prainge for thy foes
  may plaint within my breaste
Such charities, as from my hart,
  I malis maye deteste.

Graunt y^t thy pearced handes, which did
    of nothing all thinges frame,
May move me to lift my handes,
    and ever praise thy name. . . .

Graunt y^t thie rising up from death
    may rayse my thoughts from sinne:
Graunt y^t thy parting from this earth
    from earthe my hart may winne.

Graunt lord y^t thy assendinge then
    may lift my mynde to thee.
That there my hart and joye may reste,
    though heare in flesh I be.

PHILIP HOWARD

Blessed Philip Howard, Earl of Arundel (1557–1595),
was imprisoned because of his Catholicism and political
opinions during the reign of Elizabeth. He died in
prison.

§ 3

Beloved Pan, and all ye other gods who haunt this place,
give me beauty in the inward soul; and may the outward and
inward man be at one. May I reckon the wise to be the
wealthy, and may I have such a quantity of gold as a temper-
ate man and he only can bear and carry—Anything more?
This prayer, I think, is enough for me.

SOCRATES

This prayer is ascribed to Socrates in Plato's *Phaedrus*.
It is addressed to Pan, because it was spoken on the bank
of the river Ilissus, and Pan, in Greek mythology, was
god of the countryside. Socrates was scrupulous in
respecting the current órthodoxy, but, as depicted by
Plato, was in fact one of the purest monotheists in the
history of religion.

Give me neither poverty nor riches; feed me with food convenient for me.

THE BOOK OF PROVERBS

Strengthen me, O God, by the grace of Thy Holy Spirit; grant me to be strengthened with might in the inner man, and to put away from my heart all useless anxiety and distress, and let me never be drawn aside by various longings after anything whatever, whether it be worthless or precious; but may I regard all things as passing away, and myself as passing away with them.

Grant me prudently to avoid the one who flatters me, and patiently to bear with the one who contradicts me; for it is a mark of great wisdom not to be moved by every wind of words, nor to give ear to the wicked flattery of the siren; for thus we shall go on securely in the course we have begun.

THOMAS à KEMPIS

Thomas à Kempis, known to everyone as the reputed author of the *Imitation of Christ*, was an Augustinian monk, 1380–1471.

Our eyes may see some uncleanness, but let not our mind see things that are not clean. Our ears may hear some uncleanness, but let not our mind hear things that are not clean.

THE COMMONEST SHINTO PRAYER

See note on page 284.

This is my prayer to thee, my lord—strike, strike at the root of penury in my heart.
Give me the strength lightly to bear my joys and sorrows.
Give me the strength to make my love fruitful in service.

Give me the strength never to disown the poor or bend my
knees before insolent might.
Give me the strength to raise my mind high above daily
trifles.
And give me the strength to surrender my strength to thy
will with love.

RABINDRANATH TAGORE

O my most holy Lady, the Mother of God, by thy holy and
all-powerful prayers remove from me, thy humble and
burdened servant, despair, forgetfulness, lack of understanding and negligence, and take away all unclean, crafty,
and blameworthy thoughts from my smitten heart, and from
my darkened mind; quench the flame of my passions, for I
am poor and lost; deliver me from many cruel recollections
and undertakings, and set me free from all evil actions; for
thou art blessed of all generations, and thy most honourable
name is glorified unto the ages of ages. Amen.

EASTERN CHURCH

Give to me, O Lord, a steadfast heart, which no unworthy
affection may drag downwards; give me an unconquered
heart, which no tribulation can wear out; give me an
upright heart, which no unworthy purpose may tempt aside.
Bestow upon me also, O Lord my God, understanding to
know Thee, diligence to seek Thee, wisdom to find Thee, and
a faithfulness that may finally embrace Thee. Amen.

ST. THOMAS AQUINAS · 1225?–74

O Lord. Endue me with more contentedness in what is
present, and less solicitude about what is future; with a

patient mind to submit to any loss of what I have, or to any disappointment of what I expect.

BISHOP SIMON PATRICK

Bishop Patrick was a seventeenth-century composer of hymns.

O God, animate us to cheerfulness. May we have a joyful sense of our blessings, learn to look on the bright circumstances of our lot, and maintain a perpetual contentedness under Thy allotments. Fortify our minds against disappointments and calamity. Preserve us from despondency, from yielding to dejection. Teach us that no evil is intolerable but a guilty conscience; and that nothing can hurt us, if, with true loyalty of affection, we keep Thy commandments, and take refuge in Thee. Amen.

WILLIAM ELLERY CHANNING

Channing, the American philanthropist, divine and "apostle of Unitarianism" (1780-1842), was famous for his opposition to slavery.

God deliver us from sullen saints!

ST. TERESA OF AVILA · 1515-82

O God, the Father of our Saviour Jesus Christ, Whose name is great, Whose nature is blissful, Whose goodness is inexhaustible, God and Ruler of all things, Who art blessed forever; before Whom stand thousands and thousands, and ten thousand times ten thousand, the hosts of holy angels and archangels;

Sanctify, O Lord, our souls and bodies and spirits, search our consciences, and cast out of us every evil thought, every base desire, all envy and pride, all wrath and anger, and all that is contrary to Thy holy will. And grant us, O Lord, Lover of men, with a pure heart and contrite soul to call upon Thee, our holy God and Father who art in heaven. Amen.

THE SYRIAN RITE

The Syrian rite is one of the nine main groups of Christian liturgies.

Lord, I perceive my soul deeply guilty of envy. . . . I had rather thy work were undone than done better by another than by myself! . . . Dispossess me, Lord, of this bad spirit, and turn my envy into holy emulation; . . . yea, make other men's gifts to be mine, by making me thankful to thee for them.

THOMAS FULLER · HISTORIAN · 1608–61

God grant me
Serenity to accept the things I cannot change,
Courage to change the things I can,
And wisdom to know the difference.

UNTRACED

Oh God that bringest all things to pass, grant me the spirit of reverence for noble things.

PINDAR · GREEK POET · ABOUT 522–448 B.C.

Grant me to become noble of heart.

SOCRATES

This is from Plato's 'Phaedrus'.

Lord, give us faith that right makes might.

ABRAHAM LINCOLN

God the Father of our Lord Jesus Christ, increase us in faith and truth and gentleness, and grant us part and lot among His saints.

ST. POLYCARP

St. Polycarp, c. 69–c. 155, was Bishop of Smyrna. He was acquainted with St. John and "many others who had seen the Lord".

And still, O Lord, to me impart
An innocent and grateful heart.

COLERIDGE

Jesus Christ, Thou child so wise,
Bless mine hands and fill mine eyes,
And bring my soul to Paradise.

HILAIRE BELLOC · 1870–1953

§ 4

Grant, O Lord, that I may give Thee choice gifts,
three lighted and dazzling torches:
my spirit, my soul and my body.
My spirit to the Father,
my soul to the Son,
my body to the Holy Ghost.

O Father, sanctify my spirit!
O Son, sanctify my soul!
O Holy Ghost, sanctify my sin-soiled body!

EASTERN CHURCH

O most merciful Redeemer, Friend, and Brother,
May we know Thee more clearly,
Love Thee more dearly,
Follow Thee more nearly:
For ever and ever. Amen.

ST. RICHARD OF CHICHESTER · 1197–1253

May the strength of God pilot us.
May the power of God preserve us.
May the wisdom of God instruct us.
May the hand of God protect us.
May the way of God direct us.
May the shield of God defend us.
May the host of God guard us against the snares of evil and
the temptations of the world.
May Christ be with us.
Christ before us.
Christ in us.
Christ over us.
May Thy salvation, O Lord, be always ours this day and
forever more.

ST. PATRICK

This is part of the "Breastplate" of St. Patrick
(389?–461), believed to have been composed by him in
preparation for his victory (i.e. as a shield) against
paganism in Ireland.

Grant us, O Lord, not to set our hearts on earthly things, but to love things heavenly; and even now, while we are placed among things that are passing away, to cleave to those that shall abide; through Jesus Christ our Lord. Amen.

LEONINE SACRAMENTARY

A Sacramentary is an early form of office book in the Western Church, containing the rites and prayers belonging to the several sacraments. The *Liber Sacramentorum* from which the above is taken is usually attributed to Leo I (the Great), Pope 440–61.

Das hört ich bei Menschen am meisten bestaunen,
Dass Erde nicht war noch oben Himmel,
Noch Baum, noch irgend ein Berg nicht war,
Noch die Sonne nicht schien,
Noch der Mond nicht leuchtete,
Noch das berühmte Meer;
Dass noch nirgends nichts war am Enden und Wenden,
Und da war der eine allmächtige Gott,
Der Männer mildester:
Und da waren auch manche
Mit ihm göttliche Geister.
Gott heilig, Gott allmächtig,
Der Himmel und Erde wirktest,
Und der den Menschen so manch Gut gabst,
Gib mir in Deiner Gnade rechten Glauben,
Und guten Willen, Weisheit und Klugheit,
Und Kraft, Teufeln zu widerstehen und Arges zu vertreiben
Und Deinen Willen zu tun.

THE WESSOBRUNN PRAYER

Dating from the eighth century, this is the earliest known German prayer. It is called *Das Wessobrunner Gebet* because it was found in the monastery of Wessobrunn in Bavaria.

This I heard most marvelled at amongst men: that earth was not yet, nor the heavens above, nor tree, nor any mountain; that the sun did not shine, nor the moon; that the great sea was not there; that there was nothing anywhere, but that there was One Almighty God, the mildest of men, and there were some god-like spirits with him. O God the Holy One, O God the Almighty One, who created heaven and earth and who gave mankind so much good, give me in Thy grace the right faith, goodwill, and wisdom, and strength to withstand devils, to drive away evil and to do Thy will.

TRANSLATED BY B.G.

O God of the fathers, and Lord who keepest thy mercy, who madest all things by thy word; and by thy wisdom thou formedst man, that he should have dominion over the creatures that were made by thee, and rule the world in holiness and righteousness, and execute judgement in uprightness of soul; give me wisdom, her that sitteth by thee on thy throne; and reject me not from among thy servants: because I am thy bondman and the son of thy handmaid, a man weak and short-lived, and of small power to understand judgement and laws. For even if a man be perfect among the sons of men, yet if the wisdom that cometh from thee be not with him, he shall be held in no account. . . .

For what man shall know the counsel of God? Or who shall conceive what the Lord willeth? For the thoughts of mortals are timorous, and our devices are prone to fail. For a corruptible body weigheth down the soul, and the earthy frame lieth heavily on the mind that is full of cares. And hardly do we divine the things that are on the earth, and the things that are close at hand we find with labour; but the things that are in the heavens who ever yet traced out?

And whoever gained knowledge of thy counsel, except thou gavest wisdom, and sentest thy holy spirit from on high? And it was thus that the ways of them which are on earth were corrected, and men were taught the things that are pleasing unto thee; and through wisdom were they saved.

THE WISDOM OF SOLOMON (APOCRYPHA)

§ 5

My master hath a garden, full-filled with divers flowers,
Where thou may'st gather posies gay, all times and hours,
Here nought is heard
But paradise-bird,
Harp, dulcimer, and lute,
With cymbal
And timbrel
And the gentle sounding flute.

Oh! Jesus, Lord, my heal and weal, my bliss complete,
Make thou my heart thy garden-plot, true, fair and neat,
That I may hear
This music clear,
Harp, dulcimer, and lute,
With cymbal
And timbrel
And the gentle sounding flute.

TRADITIONAL

There follows a Coda
to this group
of prayers for ourselves:
prayers for simplicity of life

Pray God, keep us simple.

THACKERAY

Poverty was in the crib and like a faithful squire she kept herself armed in the great combat Thou didst wage for our redemption. During Thy passion she alone did not forsake Thee. Mary, Thy mother, stopped at the foot of the cross, but poverty mounted it with Thee and clasped Thee in her embrace unto the end; and when Thou wast dying of thirst, as a watchful spouse she prepared for Thee the gall. Thou didst expire in the ardour of her embraces, nor did she leave Thee when dead, O Lord Jesus, for she allowed not Thy body to rest elsewhere than in a borrowed grave.

O poorest Jesus, the grace I beg of Thee is to bestow on me the treasure of the highest poverty.

Grant that the distinctive mark of our Order may be never to possess anything as its own under the sun, for the glory of Thy name.

ST. FRANCIS OF ASSISI

O God, make me live lowly and die lowly and rise from the dead among the lowly.

MUSLIM

This is said to have been a prayer of Mohammed.

To thee, O God, we turn for peace ... but grant us too the blessed assurance that nothing shall deprive us of that peace, neither ourselves, nor our foolish earthly desires, nor my wild longings, nor the anxious cravings of my heart.

SÖREN KIERKEGAARD · 1813–55

Give me my scallop-shell of quiet,
My staff of faith to walk upon,
My scrip of joy, immortal diet,
My bottle of salvation,
My gown of Glory, hope's true gage;
And thus I'll take my pilgrimage.

SIR WALTER RALEIGH

Were a mansion of pearls erected and inlaid with gems for
   me;
Perfumed with musk, saffron, fragrant aloes and sandal to
   confer delight;
May it not be that on beholding these things I may forget
   Thee, O God, and not remember Thy name ?. . .
Were the earth to be studded with diamonds and rubies, and
   my couch to be similarly adorned;
Were fascinating damsels whose faces were decked with
   jewels to shed lustre and enhance the pleasure of the
   scene;
May it not be that on beholding them I may forget Thee and
   not remember Thy name? . . .
Were I to become a monarch on my throne and raise an
   army;
Were dominion and regal revenue mine . . . they would all be
   worthless;
May it not be that on beholding these things I may forget
   Thee and not remember Thy name?

THE JAPJI · SIKH

See note on page 284.

O God of mountains, stars, and boundless spaces,
O God of freedom and of joyous hearts,

62

When Thy face looketh forth from all men's faces,
There will be room enough in crowded marts!
Brood Thou around me, and the noise is o'er,
Thy universe my closet with shut door.

GEORGE MACDONALD · 1824–1905

I'll hope no more
For things that will not come;
And, if they do, they prove but cumbersome;
    Wealth brings much woe:
    And, since it fortunes so,
    'Tis better to be poor,
    Than so t'abound,
    As to be drownd,
Or overwhelm'd with store.

Pale care, avant,
I'll learn to be content
With that small stock, Thy bounty gave or lent.
    What may conduce
    To my most healthful use,
    Almighty God, me grant;
    But that, or this,
    That hurtful is
Deny Thy suppliant.

ROBERT HERRICK · 1591–1674

    Let me love Thee so that the honour, riches and pleasures
of the world may seem unworthy even of hatred—may be
not even encumbrances.

COVENTRY PATMORE · 1823–1896

2

O, to have a little house!
  To own the hearth and stool and all!
The heaped-up sods upon the fire,
  The pile of turf against the wall!

And I am praying to God on high,
  And I am praying Him night and day.
For a little house, a house of my own—
  Out of the wind's and rain's way.

PADRAIC COLUM · CONTEMPORARY

There follows a second Coda
to this group
of prayers for ourselves:
prayers for protection

Autumn hath all the summer's fruitful treasure;
Gone is our sport, fled is poor Croyden's pleasure:
Short days, sharp days, long nights come on apace,
Ah, who shall hide us from the winter's face?
Cold doth increase, the sickness will not cease,
And here we lie, God knows, with little ease.
From winter, plague, and pestilence, good Lord, deliver us!

London doth mourn, Lambeth is quite forlorn,
Trades cry, woe worth that ever they were born:
The want of term is town and city's harm;
Close chambers we do want, to keep us warm,
Long banished must we live from our friends:
This low-built house will bring us to our ends.
From winter, plague, and pestilence, good Lord, deliver us!

THOMAS NASHE · 1567–1601

Nashe, poet, playwright and pamphleteer, was a friend
of Marlowe.

DAS HIRTEN-AVE MARIA

Juhu! Juhu!
Ave Maria!
Gott Vater, Du Schöpfer von Himmel und Erd',
Beschirm unsern Ring, behüt unsern Herd!
Unsere liebe Frau mit ihrem Kind,
Breite den Schutzmantel über Alp und Gesind!
Sankt Petrus, du Wächter an der Himmelspfort',
Schütz uns vor Raubtieren, sei unser Hort!
Bann' dem Bären die Tatzen, dem Wolf den Fang,
Verschliess' dem Luchs den Zahn, dem Stein den Gang,
Sperr' dem Leuen die Bahn, dem Wurm den Schweif,
Zertritt dem Raben den Schnabel, die Kralle dem Greif!
Sankt Theodul, du heiliger Schutzpatron,
Bitte für uns bei Gott am Himmelsthron!

Sankt Sebastian, hör unser Bitten und Flehen,
Lass' kein Unglück zu Holz noch zu Stein geschehen!
Sankt Cyprian, Fürbitter in aller Not,
Bewahr' uns vor Unfall und jähem Tod!
Sankt Wendelin, Heiliger mit Hirtenstab,
Recht wende du und weise unsere Hab'!
Lieber Sankt Veit, weck' auf uns zur rechten Zeit,
Behüt uns in unserm Tal,
Allhie und allüberall!
Das gescheh' im Namen der Heiligen Dreifaltigkeit
Und in Gottes höchster Dreieinigkeit!

> Oho, behüt' uns Gott!
> Oho, behüt' uns Gott!
> Oho, behüt' uns Gott!
> Juhu! Juhu!

This has been sung from the mountain tops in Liechtenstein every summer evening for hundreds of years, and still is.

THE COWHERDS' AVE MARIA:
Translation of the above

> Juhu! Juhu!
> Ave Maria!

God Father, creator of heaven and earth,
Shelter our enclosures, protect our hearth!
Dear our Lady with your child in your arm,
Spread Thy cloak o'er us, keep us from harm!
St. Peter, heaven's guardian by night and by day,
Be our protector from all beasts of prey!
Lock the wolf's tooth, ban the bear's paw,
Stop the roll of the stone and the lynx' jaw,
Bar the lion's path and the dragon's tail,
Crush the raven's beak and the griffin's flail.
Thou patron Saint, holy St. Theodul,

Pray for us all at God's holy throne.
St. Sebastian, hear our supplication and word,
Save us from misfortune through stone or wood.
St. Cyprian, mediator in every distress,
Protect us from accident and sudden death.
St. Wendelin, Saint with the shepherd's staff,
Advise and guide wisely all that we have.
Dear St. Veit, wake us when the hour is right,
Guard us in our valley,
Here and everywhere.
This we beg in the name of the Father and Son,
And Holy Ghost, the Three in One!

Oho, protect us O Father!
Oho, protect us O Father!
Oho, protect us O Father!
Juhu! Juhu!

TRANSLATED BY B.G.

THE FISHERMEN'S PRAYER

Protégez moi, mon Seigneur,
Ma barque est si petite,
Et votre mer est si grande.

OLD BRETON

Translation:

Protect me, O Lord;
My boat is so small,
And your sea is so big.

FIRST PART

IV. FOR NEIGHBOURS AND "ENEMIES"

MEDITATION

Show love to all creatures, and thou wilt be happy; for when thou lovest all things, thou lovest the Lord, for he is all in all.

TULSI DAS · 1532–1623 · HINDU

Although I am far from Thee, may no one else be far from Thee.

HAFIZ · DIED 1388 · PERSIAN POET

What hast Thou done for me? In every soul whom Thou hast created, Thou has given me the Similitude of Thyself to enjoy! Could my desires have aspired unto such treasures?

THOMAS TRAHERNE

Lord! thou art the Hindu, the Moslem, the Turk and the Feringhi; thou art the Persian, the Sanskritian, the Arabian;
Thou art the speech . . . Thou art the warrior clad in shining armour, and thou art the peace supreme!
Thou art man, woman, child and God!
Thou art the flute player, the herdsman that goes grazing his dumb cows!
Thou bestoweth love and thou givest thyself to all!
Thou art the protector of life and the giver of all prosperity!
Thou art the cure of all sorrow and suffering.
In all shapes and everywhere, thou art dear to me; in every form thou art thyself!
Thou art my vow . . . my beginning and my end.

GOVIND SINGH · 17TH CENTURY · SIKH

See note on page 284.

Grant us that we may never forget, O Lord, that every man is the son of a King.

HASIDIC

See note on page 281.

O my God, guard my tongue from evil and my lips from speaking guile; and to such as curse me let my soul be dumb, yea, let my soul be to all as the dust.

THE HEBREW PRAYER BOOK

Be Thou praised, O Lord, for those who forgive for love of thee, and bear sufferings and tribulations.

Blessed are they who are steadfast in peace, for by thee, Most High, shall they be crowned.

ST. FRANCIS OF ASSISI

May it be Thy will, O Lord, that no man foster hatred against us in his heart, and that we foster no hatred in our hearts against any man; that no man foster envy of us in his heart, and that we foster no envy in our hearts of any man.

THE TALMUD

The Talmud is a great collection of Rabbinical treatises, etc., reduced to writing in the early centuries of our era.

As the first martyr Stephen prayed to thee for his murderers, O Lord, so we fall before thee and pray: forgive all who hate and maltreat us and let not one of them perish because of us, but may all be saved by thy grace, O God the all-bountiful.

EASTERN CHURCH

O Lord, the Author and Persuador of peace, love and goodwill, soften our hard and steely hearts, warm our frozen and icy hearts, that we may wish well to one another, and may be the true disciples of Jesus Christ. And give us grace even now to begin to show forth that heavenly life, wherein there is no hatred, but peace and love on all hands, one toward another. Amen.

LUDOVICUS VIVES · 1492–1540

Ludovicus Vives was a Spanish scholar, a friend of Erasmus, and reputedly tutor to Mary, daughter of Henry VIII.

I offer up unto Thee my prayers and intercessions, for those especially who have in any matter hurt, grieved, or found fault with me, or who have done me any damage or displeasure.

For all those also whom, at any time, I have vexed, troubled, burdened, and scandalized, by words or deeds, knowingly or in ignorance: that Thou wouldst grant us all equally pardon for our sins, and for our offences against each other.

Take away from our hearts, O Lord, all suspiciousness, indignation, wrath and contention, and whatsoever may hurt charity, and lessen brotherly love. Have mercy, O Lord, have mercy on those that crave Thy mercy, give grace unto them that stand in need thereof, and make us such that we may be worthy to enjoy Thy grace, and go forward to life eternal. Amen.

THOMAS à KEMPIS

Almighty God, have mercy on N and N and on all that bear me evil will, and would me harm, and their faults and mine together, by such easy, tender, merciful means as Thine infinite wisdom best can divine, vouchsafe to amend and redress, and make us saved souls in heaven together where we may ever live and love together with thee and thy blessed saints, O glorious Trinity, for the bitter passion of our sweet saviour Christ. Amen.

ASCRIBED TO SIR THOMAS MORE

CHRISTIAN PRAYER FOR OUR ENEMIES

Most merciful and loving Father,

We beseech Thee most humbly, even with all our hearts,

To pour out upon our enemies with bountiful hands whatsoever things Thou knowest may do them good.

And chiefly a sound and uncorrupt mind,

Where-through they may know Thee and love Thee in true
charity and with their whole heart,

And love us, Thy children, for Thy sake.

Let not their first hating of us turn to their harm,

Seeing that we cannot do them good for want of ability.

Lord, we desire their amendment and our own.

Separate them not from us by punishing them,

But join and knot them to us by Thy favourable dealings with
them.

And, seeing we be all ordained to be citizens of the one
everlasting city,

Let us begin to enter into that way here already by mutual
love,

Which may bring us right forth thither.

ELIZABETHAN

HEBREW PRAYER FOR OUR ENEMIES

O Lord our God and God of our Fathers, we pray that,
in this moment of victory, we may remember the legend
handed down to us by our Doctors: that when, after the
crossing of the Red Sea, Miriam raised her voice in exultation, and the angels at the Throne of Thy Glory began to take
up the refrain, Thou didst rebuke them, saying: "What!
My children are drowning, and you would sing?"

Many years ago, when destroying some old papers, I
came across this prayer in faded pencil, and copied it
out. It was headed "Armistice Day", and was written in

78

a hand unknown to me. I think its author may have been a friend of my parents who ministered in a provincial synagogue, and whom I remember as a man of great gentleness. ¶ The earliest reference to the legend itself is, I believe, by Rabbi Johanan, who died in A.D. 279. V.G.

1933-1945

May all who have done wickedness to the children of Israel in these latter days come to their rest.

YISROEL BEN AVROHOM

FIRST PART

V. FOR SUFFERERS

MEDITATION

Why has our sincere prayer for each other such great power over others? Because of the fact that by cleaving to God during prayer I become one spirit with Him, and unite with myself, by faith and love, those for whom I pray; for the Holy Ghost acting in me also acts at the same time in them, for He accomplishes all things. "We, being many, are one bread, one body." "There is one body and one Spirit."

JOHN OF CRONSTADT · RUSSIAN PRIEST · 1829–1908

FOR ALL SUFFERERS

Watch Thou, dear Lord, with those who wake, or watch, or weep to-night, and give Thine angels charge over those who sleep.

Tend Thy sick ones, O Lord Christ; rest Thy weary ones; bless Thy dying ones; soothe Thy suffering ones; shield Thy joyous ones; and all for Thy Love's sake.

ST. AUGUSTINE

FOR THE SAME

O Lord God our heavenly Father, regard, we beseech thee, with thy divine pity the pains of all thy children, and grant that the passion of our Lord and his infinite merits may make fruitful for good the miseries of the innocent, the sufferings of the sick, and the sorrows of the bereaved; through him who suffered in our flesh and died for our sake, thy Son our Saviour Jesus Christ.

SCOTTISH BOOK OF COMMON PRAYER

FOR THE COMFORTLESS

O Jesus, Du hast in Deiner Ölbergverlassenheit und Todesangst um Trost zum himmlischen Vater gebetet.

Du weisst, es gibt Seelen, die auf Erden keine Stütze, keinen Tröster haben. Sende ihnen einen Engel, der ihnen Freude gibt!

OLD GERMAN PRAYER

Translation:

O Jesus, in Thy great loneliness on the Mount of Olives, and in Thy agony, Thou didst pray to the Heavenly Father for comfort. Thou knowest that there are souls on earth who are without support and without comforters. Send them an angel to give them joy.

TRANSLATED BY B.G.

FOR THE POOR

But beggars about midsummer go breadless to supper,
And winter is yet worse, for they are wet-shod wanderers,
Frozen and famished and foully challenged
And berated by rich men so that it is rueful to listen.
Now Lord, send them summer or some manner of happi-
ness
After their going hence for what they have here suffered.
For thou mightest have made us equal, none meaner than
another,
With equal wit and wisdom, if such had been thy wishes.
Have ruth on these rich men who reward not thy prisoners;
Many are *ingrati* of the good that thou hast given them.
But God, in thy goodness, grant them grace of amendment.
For they dread no dearth nor drought nor freshets,
Nor heat nor hail, if they have their comfort.
Nothing is wanting to them here of what they wish and
will.
But poor people, thy prisoners, Lord, in the pit of misery,
Comfort thy creatures who have such a care to suffer
Through dearth, through drought, all their days here.
Woe in winter for want of clothing!
Who seldom in summer-time sup fully!
Comfort thy careworn, Christ, in thy riches.

FROM PIERS PLOWMAN · 14TH CENTURY

FOR PRISONERS AND THE CONDEMNED

O Lord God our heavenly Father, put love into our hearts,
we beseech thee, for all who lie in prison, and especially for

those who are under sentence of death; and grant that our love may bring them some measure of assuagement. Through the infinite merits of Him who bade us not to judge and Himself condemned not, and in whose Passion all men are brothers. Amen.

CONTEMPORARY BRITISH

FOR THE FORGOTTEN

Let us never forget, O Lord, the innocent victims of man's inhumanity to man: the millions who were destroyed in the gas chambers and in the holocaust of Hiroshima and Nagasaki, and the few who survived, scarred in mind or body; the uncounted numbers all over the earth who will never have enough to eat, and who, through poverty or ignorance, must watch their children die of hunger; the lepers and the cripples, and the countless others who will live out their lives in illness or disease for which they are given no relief; all who suffer because of their race or their creed or the colour of their skins; and all the children who, in their weakness, are torn from their parents and robbed of the loving care which is their birth-right. Help us, as we go unheedingly about our daily lives, to remember those who silently call to us; and to remember also that, though the need of those in distress is so vast and of such an infinite complexity, it is by the steadfast effort of individuals that it must be conquered.

CONTEMPORARY AMERICAN

FOR THE OUTRAGED DEAD

Oh Thou for whom there is neither past nor future, and in whom we all have our being eternally, help us, we pray Thee, to remember at this hour the afflicted of every nation and age, and more especially those who have been wounded, killed and tortured in war: vouchsafe that our love may bring relief to their agonies: and grant also that their persecutors may be at peace, in the name of Him who forever begs Thy forgiveness for those who torment Him on the Cross, inasmuch as they know not what they do. Amen.

CONTEMPORARY BRITISH

IN THE NAME OF CHRIST'S PASSION

O Christ, I see thy crown of thorns in every eye, thy bleeding, naked, wounded body in every soul; thy death liveth in every memory; thy crucified Person is embalmed in every affection; thy pierced feet are bathed in everyone's tears; and it is my privilege to enter with thee into every soul.

THOMAS TRAHERNE

FIRST PART

VI. FOR ANIMALS

MEDITATIONS

Seest thou the little winged fly, smaller than a grain of sand?
It has a heart like thee, a brain open to heaven & hell,
Withinside wondrous & expansive: its gates are not clos'd:
I hope thine are not: hence it clothes itself in rich array:
Hence thou art cloth'd with human beauty, O thou mortal
    man.

   *   *   *

For not one sparrow can suffer & the whole Universe not
    suffer also
In all its Regions, and its Father & Saviour not pity &
    weep.

BLAKE

  O happy living things! no tongue
  Their beauty might declare:
  A spring of love gushed from my heart,
  And I blessed them unaware.

  The selfsame moment I could pray;
  And from my neck so free
  The Albatross fell off and sank
  Like lead into the sea . . .

  Farewell, farewell! but this I tell
  To thee, thou Wedding-Guest!
  He prayeth well, who loveth well
  Both man and bird and beast.

  He prayeth best, who loveth best
  All things both great and small;
  For the dear God who loveth us,
  He made and loveth all.

COLERIDGE

Blessed art thou, O Lord our God, King of the universe, who hast such as these in thy world.

THE HEBREW PRAYER BOOK

It is prescribed in the Hebrew prayer book that this blessing should be said at the sight of beautiful animals.

Praised be thou, O Lord, who hast made every animal wise in the instinct thou has given it.

ST. ADAMNAN

Based on a sentence (translated by Helen Waddell) in the Life of St. Columba written about 690 by St. Adamnan, abbot of Iona.

O heavenly Father, protect and bless all things that have breath: guard them from all evil and let them sleep in peace.

ALBERT SCHWEITZER WHEN A CHILD

Schweitzer writes: "As far back as I can remember I was saddened by the amount of misery I saw in the world around me. One thing that especially saddened me was that unfortunate animals had to suffer so much pain and misery. It was quite incomprehensible to me why in my evening prayers I should pray for human beings only. So when my mother had prayed with me and kissed me good night, I used to add silently [the above] prayer that I had composed myself for all living creatures."

When I travel in my coach to teach thy Law, give me thought for the mare that carries me, and guard her from my impatience: when I walk through thy woods, may my right foot and my left foot be harmless to the little creatures that move in its grasses: as it is said by the mouth of thy prophet, They shall not hurt nor destroy in all my holy mountain, Amen.

RABBI MOSHE HAKOTUN

The man who taught me Hebrew ascribed this prayer, and several others, to Rabbi Moshe Hakotun ("Rabbi Moses the Small"), whom, however, I have been unable to find in any work of reference. It is possible that he was meant by my teacher to typify the Hasidic movement (see note on page 281). ¶ In the eighteenth century Rabbis often travelled long distances by coach to "teach the Law"—i.e. take divine service on the Sabbath—as guests of congregations other than their own. In their anxiety to arrive by Sabbath eve (travelling on the Sabbath being unthinkable) they may have been tempted sometimes to over-drive their horses. V.G.

For those, O Lord, the humble beasts, that bear with us the burden and heat of the day, and offer their guileless lives for the well-being of their countries: we supplicate Thy tenderness of heart, for Thou hast promised to save both man and beast, and great is Thy loving kindness, O Master, Saviour of the world.

EASTERN CHURCH

Hear our humble prayer, O God, for our friends the animals, Thy creatures. We pray especially for all that are suffering in any way; for the overworked and underfed, the hunted, lost or hungry; for all in captivity or ill-treated, and for those that must be put to death.

We entreat for them Thy mercy and pity; and for those who deal with them we ask a heart of compassion, gentle hands and kindly words.

Make us all to be true friends to animals and so more worthy followers of our merciful Saviour, Jesus Christ.

AUTHORSHIP DOUBTFUL

> The late Bishop Kirk of Oxford, writing in his diocesan magazine (c. 1953), referred to "the very real problem created for religious thought by the sufferings of animals", and commended the above as a special collect "eminently proper for any Christian to use". It is printed, without ascription, in the Rodborough Bede Book: it is also ascribed to F. L. Ghey.

Lord, may I love all Thy creation, the whole and every grain of sand in it. May I love every leaf, every ray of Thy light. May I love the animals: Thou hast given them the rudiments of thought and joy untroubled. Let me not trouble it, let me not harass them, let me not deprive them of their happiness, let me not work against Thine intent. For I acknowledge unto Thee that all is like an ocean, all is flowing and blending, and that to withhold any measure of love from anything in Thy universe is to withhold that same measure from Thee.

ADAPTED FROM DOSTOEVSKY

> From "The Conversations and Exhortations of Father Zossima" from *The Brothers Karamazov*.

O Thou who lovest Thy whole creation, give us strength, we beseech Thee, to put an end to the pain and fear of Thy hunted beasts, the same which they suffer for the careless pleasure of men: in the name of Him who said that no sparrow falls on the ground without the Father, Amen.

CONTEMPORARY BRITISH

FOR MOTHS

When
—At the mid of moon,
At end of day—
My lamp is lit,
Grant me a boon,
I pray,
And do
So order it

—That the small creatures,
Terrified and blind;
The gold and silvern moths
Of lovely kind,
Do not whirl to my taper,
Nor, therein,
Die, painfully,
And bring my light
To sin.

My light
is innocent!
Grant
—That it may be
Harmless,
And helpful,
And remarked
Of Thee.

JAMES STEPHENS · 1882–1950

AT MILKING TIME

Bless, O God, my little cow,
  Bless, O God, my desire;
Bless Thou my partnership
  And the milking of my hands, O God!

Bless, O God, each teat,
  Bless, O God, each finger;
Bless Thou each drop
  That goes into my pitcher, O God!

GAELIC

KINGFISHERS AND JACKDAWS

Let Hushim rejoice with the King's Fisher, who is of royal
  beauty, tho' plebeian size . . .
Let Mizbar rejoice with the Cadess, as is their number, so are
  their names, blessed be the Lord Jesus for them all.
For the names and number of animals are as the names and
  number of the stars . . .
Let Cherub rejoice with the Cherub who is a bird and a
  blessed Angel.
For I bless God for every feather from the wren in the sedge
  to the Cherubs and their mates . . .

CHRISTOPHER SMART · 1722–71

King's Fisher = kingfisher; cadess = jackdaw.

FOR BIRDS

I listen with reverence to the birdsong cascading
At dawn from the oasis, for it seems to me
There is no better evidence for the existence of God
Than in the bird that sings, though it knows not why,
From a spring of untrammeled joy that wells up in its heart.
Therefore I pray that no sky-hurled hawk may come
Plummeting down,
To silence the singer, and disrupt the Song.
That rhapsodic, assured, transcending song
Which foretells and proclaims, when the Plan is worked out,
Life's destiny: the joyous, benign Intention of God.

AN ARAB CHIEFTAIN

The above was sent to me by Mrs E. B. Wayne in New Zealand, who wrote: "During a motoring holiday in North Africa, we were lucky enough to spend a few days as the guests of an Arab chieftain and his French wife; their house was on the outskirts of a Libyan oasis. A feature of the early mornings there was the dawn chorus of birds, and our host expressed himself one day about this in a sort of prose-poem, which I am sending you, more or less literally translated."   v.g.

TRIBUTE TO BEES

Late on the night of Holy Saturday, in the Roman ritual, the Paschal candle (representing the risen Christ: the Greek letters alpha and omega, symbol of the Godhead, are incised on it) is carried in procession, set in the middle of the sanctuary, and praised in a great sweeping *Exsultet*, possibly composed by St. Ambrose. The following tribute to the bees comes near its close. In the *Exsultet* as at present used, the passage about bees ends with the words "this precious candle": but in an earlier text a long paragraph of eulogy follows, beginning with a Virgilian description of honey-making, continuing with the exclamation "O truly blessed and marvellous mother-bee!", and concluding with a comparison of this lady with the Virgin. (The translation is by Rev. J. B. O'Connell and H. P. R. Finberg.)

In thanksgiving for this night, then, holy Father, receive the evening sacrifice of this flame, which Holy Church, by the hands of her ministers, renders to thee in the solemn offering of this wax candle wrought by bees. For now we see the splendour of this column, kindled to the glory of God from shining flame: a flame which though it be divided into parts, yet suffers no loss of light, being fed from the ever-melting wax that the mother-bee brought forth to form the substance of this precious candle. . . . O truly blessed and marvellous mother-bee! . . .

FIRST PART

VII. FOR THE NATION AND THE
WORLD

MEDITATION

If he might have had but one request of God Almighty, it should have been, above all other, that he might be a blessing to mankind. That was his daily prayer above all his petitions. He wisely knew that it included all petitions; for he that is a blessing to mankind must be blessed, that he may be so, and must inherit all their affections, and in that their treasures.

THOMAS TRAHERNE

O Lord, vouchsafe to look mercifully upon us, and grant
that we may ever choose the way of peace.

SARUM MISSAL

The Sarum Missal was a widespread liturgy of the
pre-reformation English Church.

May God bless youth! And I pray Thee, Lord, send peace
and light to Thy people.

DOSTOEVSKY

Lord of the world, I beg of you to redeem Israel. And if
you do not want to do that, then redeem the Gentiles.

ISRAEL OF KOZNITZ · DIED 1814 · HASID

I pray God the Omnipotent to place us in the ranks of
those . . . in whom he inspires fervour lest they forget Him;
whom He cleanses from all defilement, that nothing may
remain in them except Himself; yea, of those whom he in-
dwells completely, that they may adore none beside him.

AL-GHAZALI · 1059–1111 · SUFI

See note on page 286.

FOR ERIN

Three things are of the Evil One:
    An evil eye;
    An evil tongue;
    An evil mind.

Three things are of God, and these three are what Mary told her son, for she heard them in Heaven;

The merciful word,
The singing word,
And the good word.

May the power of these three holy things be on all men and women of Erin for ever. Amen.

TRADITIONAL IRISH

FOR MEXICO

O merciful Lord, let this chastisement with which thou hast visited us, the people, be as those which a father or mother inflicts on their children, not out of anger, but to the end that they may be free from follies and vices.

ANCIENT MEXICAN

FOR ISRAEL

O Lord, the great and dreadful God. . . .

We have sinned, and have committed iniquity, and have done wickedly, and have rebelled, even by departing from thy precepts and from thy judgements. . . .

O Lord, to us belongeth confusion of face, to our kings, to our princes, and to our fathers, because we have sinned against thee. . . .

Now therefore, O our God, hear the prayer of thy servant, and his supplications, and cause thy face to shine upon thy sanctuary that is desolate, for the Lord's sake.

O my God, incline thine ear and hear; open thine eyes and behold our desolations, . . . for we do not present our supplications before thee for our righteousnesses, but for thy great mercies.

O Lord, hear; O Lord, forgive; O Lord, hearken and do.

THE BOOK OF DANIEL

A STATESMAN'S PRAYER

God, grant that no word may fall from us, against our will, unfit for the present need.

PERICLES

A QUEEN'S PRAYER

O Lorde God Father everlasting, which reigneth over the Kingdoms of men . . . so teach me, I humbly beseech Thee, thy word, and so strengthen me with thy grace that I may feed thy people with a faithful and a true heart: and rule them prudently with power. Oh Lord, thou hast set me on high, my flesh is frail and weak. If I therefore at any time forget thee, touch my heart, o Lord, that I may again remember thee. If I swell against thee, pluck me down in my own conceit . . . I acknowledge, oh my King, without thee my throne is unstable, my seat unsure, my Kingdom tottering, my life uncertain. I see all things in this life subject to mutability, nothing to continue still at one stay . . . Create therefore in me, o Lord, a new heart, and so renew my spirit within me that thy law may be my study, thy truth my delight; thy church my care; thy people my crown; thy righteousness my pleasure; thy service my government . . . So shall this my kingdom through thee be established with peace . . .

QUEEN ELIZABETH I

According to Frederick Chamberlin's *The Sayings of Queen Elizabeth* (John Lane, The Bodley Head, 1923), this is from a little book in which she wrote down her religious thoughts. It was three inches high by two inches wide, of sixty-five vellum pages, bound in shagreen, with two gold clips, each mounted with a ruby. The original disappeared about seventy years ago, but the last known owner had had some copies made of it.

AN ARCHBISHOP'S PRAYER

Lord, bless this kingdom, that religion and virtue may season all sorts of men: that there may be peace within our gates, and prosperity in all our borders. In time of trouble guide us, and in peace may we not forget Thee; and whether in plenty or in want, may all things be so ordered, that we may patiently and peaceably seek Thy Kingdom and its righteousness, the only full supply and sure foundation both of men and states; so that we may continue a place and people to do Thee service to the end of time.

WILLIAM LAUD · 1573–1645

See note on page 288.

THE KNIGHTS' PRAYER

O God, Almighty Father, King of kings and Lord of all rulers, grant that the hearts and minds of all who go out as leaders before us, the statesmen, the judges, the men of learning and the men of wealth, may be so filled with the love of Thy laws and of that which is righteous and life-giving, that they may serve as a wholesome salt unto the earth, and be worthy stewards of Thy good and perfect gifts, through Jesus Christ our Lord.

DOUBTFUL

See note on page 288.

THE COMMONS' PRAYER

Almighty God, by whom alone Kings reign, and Princes decree justice; and from whom alone cometh all counsel, wisdom, and understanding; We thine unworthy servants, here gathered together in thy Name, do most humbly beseech thee to send down thy Heavenly Wisdom from above, to direct and guide us in all our consultations: And grant that, we having thy fear always before our eyes, and laying aside all private interests, prejudices, and partial affections, the result of all our counsels may be the glory of thy blessed Name, the maintenance of true Religion and Justice, the safety, honour, and happiness of the Queen, the publick welfare, peace and tranquillity of the Realm, and the uniting and knitting together of the hearts of all persons and estates within the same, in true Christian Love and Charity one towards another, through Jesus Christ our Lord and Saviour. Amen.

SEVENTEENTH CENTURY OR EARLIER

There is every reason to believe that this prayer, regularly used at sittings of the House, dates from at least 1661.

FOR THE SEVENTEENTH CENTURY

Yet O for his sake who sits now by thee
    All crown'd with victory,
So guide us through this Darknes, that we may
    Be more and more in love with day;

Settle, and fix our hearts, that we may move
    In order, peace, and love,
And taught obedience by thy whole Creation,
    Become an humble, holy nation.

Give to thy spouse her perfect, and pure dress,
  Beauty and holiness,
And so repair these Rents, that men may see
  And say, Where God is, all agree.

HENRY VAUGHAN · 1622–1695

FOR OUR PRESENT NEED

. . . So when the winter of the world and Man's fresh Fall
When democratic Death feared no more the heart's coldness
Shall be forgotten,
O Love, return to the dying world, as the light
Of morning, shining in all regions, latitudes
And households of high heaven within the heart. . . .

Now falls the night of the world:—O Spirit moving upon the
  waters
Your peace instil
In the animal heat and splendour of the blood—
The hot gold of the sun that flames in the night
And knows not down-going
But moves with the revolutions in the heavens.

The thunders and the fires and acclamations
Of the leaves of spring are stilled, but in the night
The Holy Ghost speaks in the whispering leaves.
O wheat-ear shining like a fire and the bright gold,
O water brought from far to the dying gardens!

Bring peace to the famine of the heart and lips,
And to the Last Man's loneliness
Of those who dream they can bring back sight to the blind!
You are the Night
When the long hunt for Nothing is at rest

·In the Blind Man's Street, and in the human breast
The hammer of Chaos is stilled.

                            Be then the sleep
When Judas gives again the childish kiss
That once his mother knew—and wash the stain
From the darkened hands of the universal Cain.

EDITH SITWELL

§ 2

O Lord, convert the world—and begin with me.

A CHINESE STUDENT'S PRAYER

FIRST PART

VIII. SPECIAL OFFICES

MEDITATION

A man should utter daily a hundred Benedictions.

RABBI MEIR · 2ND CENTURY A.D.

On going to stool:

Blessed art thou, O Lord our God, King of the universe, who hast formed man in wisdom, and created in him many orifices and vessels. It is revealed and known before the throne of thy glory, that if one of these be opened, or one of those be closed, it would be impossible to exist and to stand before thee. Blessed art thou, O Lord, who healest all flesh and doest wondrously.

THE HEBREW PRAYER BOOK

When looking at the beauties of nature:

O God who hast revealed Thyself to us not only as Truth but as Beauty, restrain us from that rude and careless haste which disregards the manifold and incessant beauty of Thy creation, whereby Thou art revealing Thyself to us: grant us the recollectedness whereby we may look on these manifest and unceasing revelations of the loveliness of Thy nature and, so looking upon these reflections of Thee, may begin to learn what Thy unveiled splendour must be, Thy formless beauty, of which all beauty of form is but a shadow.

GERALD HEARD

On seeing certain cities:

Blessed art thou, O Lord our God, King of the universe, who hast given of the wisdom of thy hands to flesh and blood, that beautiful cities might rise for thy glory.

RABBI MOSHE HAKOTUN

This is said to have been written in Venice.

On seeing trees blossoming for the first time in the year:

Blessed art thou, O Lord our God, King of the universe, who hast made thy world lacking in nought, but hast produced therein goodly creatures and goodly trees wherewith to give delight unto the children of men.

THE HEBREW PRAYER BOOK

On smelling certain herbs:

Blessed art thou, O Lord our God, King of the universe, who with the scent of this lowly herb transportest the soul.

RABBI MOSHE HAKOTUN

On seeing deformed persons:

Blessed art Thou, O Lord our God, King of the universe, who variest the forms of thy creatures.

THE HEBREW PRAYER BOOK

After listening to music:

Blessed art Thou, O Lord, who hast revealed thyself in music, and granted me the love of it.

CONTEMPORARY HEBREW

On tasting any fruit for the first time in the season; on entering into possession of a new house; on wearing new clothes; on birthdays; and on any occasion for special rejoicing:

Blessed art thou, O Lord our God, King of the universe,

who hast kept us in life, and hast preserved us, and hast
enabled us to reach this season.

THE HEBREW PRAYER BOOK

*From the wedding service; and for remembrance in
old age by the married:*

Blessed art thou, O Lord our God, King of the universe,
who hast created joy and gladness, bridegroom and bride,
mirth and exultation, pleasure and delight, love, brotherhood,
peace and fellowship. Blessed art thou, O Lord, who makest
the bridegroom to rejoice with the bride.

THE HEBREW PRAYER BOOK

At a baptism:

Thou Being who inhabitest the heights
Imprint Thy blessing betimes,
Remember Thou the child of my body,
In Name of the Father of peace;
When the priest of the King
On him puts the water of meaning,
Grant him the blessing of the Three
    Who fill the heights.
  The blessing of the Three
    Who fill the heights.

Sprinkle down upon him Thy grace,
Give Thou to him virtue and growth,
Give Thou to him strength and guidance,
Give Thou to him flocks and possessions,
Sense and reason void of guile,
Angel wisdom in his day,

That he may stand without reproach
    In Thy presence.
He may stand without reproach
    In Thy presence.

GAELIC

"Immediately after its birth," explained the crofter who
recited this prayer to Dr. Carmichael (see note on page
287), "the nurse or other person present drops three
drops of water on the forehead of the child. The first
drop is in the name of the Father, representing wisdom;
the second drop is in the name of the Son, representing
peace; the third drop is in the name of the Spirit, representing purity."

At a circumcision:

Blessed be he that cometh.
O give thanks unto the Lord; for he is good; for his
loving-kindness endureth for ever. This little child, may he
become great. Even as he has entered into the covenant, so
may he enter into . . . the nuptial canopy and into good deeds.

THE HEBREW PRAYER BOOK

On seeing a child:

Lord Jesu Christ, our Lord most dear,
    As thou wast once an infant here,
So give this child of thine, we pray,
Thy grace and blessing day by day.
    O holy Jesu, Lord Divine,
    We pray thee guard this child of thine.

As in thy heavenly kingdom, Lord,
    All things obey thy sacred word,

Do thou thy mighty succour give,
And shield this child by morn and eve.
O holy Jesu, Lord Divine,
We pray thee guard this child of thine.

15TH CENTURY GERMAN HYMN

The translation is by Catherine Winkworth; the melody
was by H. von Laufenberg, and was composed about
1430.

*On the eve of the Sabbath, when parents bless their
children:*

The Lord bless thee, and keep thee: the Lord make his
face to shine upon thee, and be gracious unto thee: the Lord
lift up his countenance upon thee, and give thee peace.

THE BOOK OF NUMBERS

The passage in the Book of Numbers reads: "And the
Lord spake unto Moses, saying, Speak unto Aaron and
unto his sons, saying, On this wise ye shall bless the
children of Israel, saying unto them, The Lord bless
thee ... etc." The Benediction was used in the Temple,
and is still used in every Synagogue: it may be pronounced there only by descendants of Aaron, the
Cohens or priests, every one of whom, owing to the
Hebrew system of naming, is known. But, in Jewish
custom, anyone may bless anyone with these ancient
words, and parents do habitually so bless their children,
particularly on Friday evenings.

Blessing for a house:

The peace of God, the peace of men,
The peace of Columba kindly,
The peace of Mary mild, the loving,

The peace of Christ, King of tenderness,
  The peace of Christ, King of tenderness

Be upon each window, upon each door,
Upon each hole that lets in light,
Upon the four corners of my house,
Upon the four corners of my bed,
  Upon the four corners of my bed;

Upon each thing my eye takes in,
Upon each thing my mouth takes in,
Upon my body that is of earth
And upon my soul that came from on high,
  Upon my body that is of earth
  And upon my soul that came from on high.

GAELIC

For the lighting of the lamps:

Praise God who sends us the light of heaven.

George Herbert, in 1631, recorded the saying of this
blessing at the lighting of the lamps as an old custom—
"and the parson likes this very much. Light is a great
blessing, and as great as food, for which we give thanks".

On kindling fire:

I will kindle my fire this morning
In presence of the holy angels of heaven,
In presence of Ariel of the loveliest form,
In presence of Uriel of the myriad charms,
Without malice, without jealousy, without envy,
Without fear, without terror of any one under the sun,
But the Holy Son of God to shield me.

Without malice, without jealousy, without envy,
Without fear, without terror of any one under the
    sun,
But the Holy Son of God to shield me.

God, kindle Thou in my heart within
A flame of love to my neighbour,
To my foe, to my friend, to my kindred all,
To the brave, to the knave, to the thrall,
O Son of the loveliest Mary,
From the lowliest thing that liveth,
To the Name that is highest of all.

GAELIC

For times of trouble:

Praised be thou, O Lord, that our spirits are comfortable,
though our present condition is as it is.

OLIVER CROMWELL

This is adapted from one of Cromwell's letters.

In moments of weariness:

Blessed art thou, O Lord our God, King of the universe,
who givest strength to the weary.

THE HEBREW PRAYER BOOK

In the same:

O Lord, Jesus Christ, Who art as the Shadow of a Great
Rock in a weary land, Who beholdest Thy weak creatures
weary of labour, weary of pleasure, weary of hope deferred,

weary of self; in Thine abundant compassion, and fellow feeling with us, and unutterable tenderness, bring us, we pray Thee, unto Thy rest. . . . Amen.

CHRISTINA ROSSETTI · 1830–94

For times of sickness:

Lord, teach me the art of patience whilst I am well, and give me the use of it when I am sick. In that day either lighten my burden or strengthen my back. Make me, who so often in my health have discovered my weakness presuming on my own strength, to be strong in my sickness when I rely solely on Thy assistance.

THOMAS FULLER

After salvation from peril:

בָּרוּךְ אַתָּה יְיָ אֱלֹהֵינוּ מֶלֶךְ הָעוֹלָם הַגּוֹמֵל לְחַיָּבִים
טוֹבוֹת שֶׁגְּמָלַנִי כָּל־טוֹב:

When an orthodox Jew has recovered from a grave physical or spiritual sickness, or has been saved from a disaster, it is customary for him to attend a synagogue service on the Sabbath and to make a public affirmation, over a scroll of the *Torah*, in the above words, which may be translated as follows: "Blessed art Thou, O Lord our God, King of the universe, who doest good to the undeserving, and hast done all good to me."

On recovering from a less serious illness:

Blessed art thou, the faithful physician unto all flesh.

THE HEBREW PRAYER BOOK

When present at a deathbed:

God, omit not this man from Thy covenant,
And the many evils which he in the body committed,
That he cannot this night enumerate.
   The many evils that he in the body committed,
   That he cannot this night enumerate.

Be this soul on Thine own arm, O Christ,
Thou King of the City of Heaven,
And since Thine it was, O Christ, to buy the soul,
At the time of the balancing of the beam,
At the time of the bringing in the judgment,
Be it now on Thine own right hand,
   Oh! on Thine own right hand.

And be the holy Michael, king of angels,
Coming to meet the soul,
And leading it home
To the heaven of the Son of God.
   The Holy Michael, high king of angels,
   Coming to meet the soul,
   And leading it home
   To the heaven of the Son of God.

GAELIC

On losing a dear one:

The Lord gave, and the Lord hath taken away; blessed be
the name of the Lord.

THE BOOK OF JOB

On awaking from sleep, after long lack of it:

Oh sleep! it is a gentle thing,
Beloved from pole to pole.

To Mary Queen the praise be given!
She sent the gentle sleep from Heaven,
That slid into my soul.

COLERIDGE

In bad weather:

Be Thou praised, my Lord, of fair weather and of all
weather.

FRANCISCAN

At a beautiful dawn, after bad weather:

O Night and Dark,
O huddled sullen clouds,
Light enters in: the sky
Whitens.
Christ comes! Depart! Depart!

The mist sheers apart
Cleft by the sun's spear.
Colour comes back to things
From his bright face.

PRUDENTIUS, TR. BY HELEN WADDELL

Prudentius, 348–c.410, was the most remarkable of the
earlier Christian poets of the West.

Before beginning a journey:

O Christ, who art the way and the truth, send now thy
guardian Angel to go with thy servants, as once thou didst
send him to Tobias, and for thy glory keep them safe and

sound from all harm and evil by the prayers of the Mother
of God, O thou who alone lovest mankind.

EASTERN CHURCH

For a like occasion:

Bless to me, O God,
   The earth beneath my foot,
Bless to me, O God,
   The path whereon I go;
Bless to me, O God,
   The thing of my desire;
     Thou Evermore of evermore,
   Bless Thou to me my rest.

Bless to me the thing
   Whereon is set my mind,
Bless to me the thing
   Whereon is set my love;
Bless to me the thing
   Whereon is set my hope;
    O Thou King of kings
   Bless Thou to me mine eye!

GAELIC

For a mother, to children going on a journey:

Be the great God between thy two shoulders
To protect thee in thy going and in thy coming,
Be the Son of Mary Virgin near thine heart,
And be the perfect Spirit upon thee pouring—
Oh, the perfect Spirit upon thee pouring!

GAELIC

"These lines," explained the crofter's wife who recited
them to Dr. Carmichael (see note on page 287), "are

whispered into the ears of sons and daughters when leaving their homes in the Outer Isles for the towns of the south and for foreign lands."

On entering a prison for any purpose:

Blessed art thou, O Lord our God, King of the universe, who loosenest the bound.

THE HEBREW PRAYER BOOK

At reaping:

God, bless Thou Thyself my reaping,
Each ridge, and plain, and field,
Each sickle curved, shapely, hard,
Each ear and handful in the sheaf,
    Each ear and handful in the sheaf.

Bless each maiden and youth,
Each woman and tender youngling,
Safeguard them beneath Thy shield of strength,
And guard them in the house of the saints,
    Guard them in the house of the saints.

Encompass each goat, sheep and lamb,
Each cow and horse, and store,
Surround Thou the flocks and herds,
And tend them to a kindly fold,
    Tend them to a kindly fold.

For the sake of Michael head of hosts,
Of Mary fair-skinned branch of grace,
Of Bride smooth-white of ringleted locks,
Of Columba of the graves and tombs,
    Columba of the graves and tombs.

GAELIC

A Grace:

Some ha'e meat, and canna eat,
    And some wad eat that want it;
But we ha'e meat, and we can eat,
    And sae the Lord be thankit.

ROBERT BURNS

Another Grace:

No ordinary meal—a sacrament awaits us
On our tables daily spread,
For men are risking lives on sea and land
That we may dwell in safety and be fed.

SCOTTISH

Before studying a language:

Lord, give wit and wisdom wisely to work,
Might and mind of right meaning
To make translation trusty and true.

JOHN TREVISA

John Trevisa translated an encyclopaedia from Latin
into English at the end of the fourteenth century.

On successfully completing an experiment, etcetera:

How admirable is thy Justice, O thou First Mover! Thou
hast not willed that any power should lack the processes or
qualities necessary for its results!

LEONARDO DA VINCI

On the receipt of flattery, adulation, or any kind of honour:

You and I know, O Lord, that I do not merit these titles of honour. But since so many good men believe them in all sincerity, I beseech Thee to aid me to avoid the snares of Satan, so that these men may not feel shame.

RABBI DAVID TALNER · HASID

On the same:

I thank Thee, Lord, for knowing me better than I know myself, and for letting me know myself better than others know me.

Make me, I pray Thee, better than they suppose, and forgive me for what they do not know.

ABU BEKR

Abu Bekr, ?572–634, was Mohamet's father-in-law, and the first Calif of Islam. It is said that he recited this prayer whenever he heard his people praising him.

When tempted to backbite:

Deliver my soul, O Lord, from lying lips, and from a deceitful tongue.

What shall be given unto thee? or what shall be done unto thee, thou false tongue?

FROM PSALM 120

For the Church:

Remember, Lord, Thy Church, to deliver her from all evil, and to perfect her in Thy love, and gather together from the four winds her sanctified into Thy kingdom; for Thine is the power and the glory for ever.

THE DIDACHE

The Didache is an early Christian document (about A.D. 120).

On entering a place of worship:

Lord, I love the habitation of thy house, and the place where thy glory dwelleth. As for me, I will worship and bow down: I will bend the knee before the Lord, my maker. And as for me, may my prayer into thee, O Lord, be in an acceptable time: O God, in the abundance of thy loving kindness answer me in the truth of thy salvation.

THE HEBREW PRAYER BOOK

The Hebrew toast for all occasions:

To life!

FIRST PART

IX. EVENING PRAYER

MEDITATION

Stand in awe, and sin not: commune with your own heart upon your bed, and be still.

THE HEBREW PRAYER BOOK

Blessed art thou, O Lord our God, King of the universe, who makest the bands of sleep to fall upon mine eyes, and slumber upon mine eyelids. May it be thy will, O Lord my God and God of my fathers, to suffer me to lie down in peace and to let me rise up again in peace. Let not my thoughts trouble me, nor evil dreams, nor evil fancies, but let my rest be perfect before thee. Blessed art thou, O Lord, who givest light to the whole world in thy glory.

THE HEBREW PRAYER BOOK

Thou, Lord, art with me, and I will not fear.

THE HEBREW PRAYER BOOK

Keep us, Lord, so awake in the duties of our callings that we may sleep in thy peace and wake in thy glory.

JOHN DONNE · 1573–1631

Thou Being of marvels,
Shield me with might,
Thou Being of statutes
 And of stars.

Compass me this night,
Both soul and body,
Compass me this night
 And on every night.

Compass me aright
Between earth and sky,
Between the mystery of Thy laws
 And mine eye of blindness;

Both that which mine eye sees
   And that which it reads not;
Both that which is clear
   And is not clear to my devotion.

GAELIC

Thou whose nature cannot sleepe,
On my temples centry keepe;
Guard me 'gainst those watchfull foes,
Whose eyes are open while mine close.
Let no dreames my head infest,
But such as *Jacobs* temples blest.
While I do reste, my soule advance,
Make my sleepe a holy trance.
That I may, my reste being wrought,
Awake into some holy thought.
And with as active vigour runne
My course, as doth the nimble Sunne.

SIR THOMAS BROWNE · 1605–82

The above is shortened.

O Lord Jesus Christ, our Watchman and Keeper, take us to thy care: grant that, our bodies sleeping, our minds may watch in thee, and be made merry by some sight of that celestial and heavenly life, wherein thou art the King and Prince, together with the Father and the Holy Spirit, where thy angels and holy souls be most happy citizens. Oh purify our souls, keep clean our bodies, that in both we may please thee, sleeping and waking, for ever. Amen.

"CHRISTIAN PRAYERS" · 1566

Christian Prayers was compiled by the Rev. Henry Bull, Fellow of Magdalen College, Oxford. A zealot for the

Reformation, he was expelled and exiled by Mary, but restored to his college by Elizabeth. He died in 1575. His lovely book is extremely rare.

All praise to Thee, my God, this night,
For all the Blessings of the Light!
Keep me, O keep me, King of kings,
Beneath Thy own Almighty Wings.

Forgive me, Lord, for Thy dear Son,
The ill that I this day have done;
That with the World, myself and Thee,
I, ere I sleep, at peace may be.

O! may my Soul on Thee repose,
And sweet sleep my Eyelids close—
Sleep, that may me more vigorous make,
To serve my God when I awake.

THOMAS KEN · 1637–1711

Thomas Ken refused to lodge Nell Gwynne in his house when Charles II brought her to Winchester. The King admired his courage and made him Bishop of Bath.

Upon my Ryght syde y me leye,
Blesid lady, to the y pray,
Ffor the teres that ye lete[1]
Upone yowr swete sonnys feete,
Sende me grace for to slepe
And good dremys for to mete,
Slepyng, wakyng, til morowe daye bee.
Owre lorde is the frwte, owre lady is the tree;
Blessid be the blossome that sprange, lady, of the!

EARLY ENGLISH · ANONYMOUS

'shed.

May Michael be at my right hand; Gabriel at my left;
before me, Uriel; behind me, Raphael; and above my head
thy divine presence, O God.

HEBREW PRAYER BOOK

A CHILD'S PRAYER

O Lord Jesus Christ, who didst receive the children who
came to Thee, receive also from me, Thy child, this evening
prayer. Shelter me under the shadow of Thy wings, that in
peace I may lie down and sleep; and do Thou waken me in
due time, that I may glorify Thee, for Thou alone art
righteous and merciful. Amen.

EASTERN CHURCH

§ 2

GOD SPEAKS

I don't like the man who doesn't sleep, says God.
Sleep is the friend of man.
Sleep is the friend of God.
Sleep is perhaps the most beautiful thing I have created.
And I myself rested on the seventh day.
He whose heart is pure, sleeps. And he who sleeps has a pure
  heart.
That is the great secret of being as indefatigable as a child.
Of having that strength in the legs that a child has.
Those new legs, those new souls,
And to begin afresh every morning, ever new,
Like young hope, new hope . . .
He who doesn't sleep is unfaithful to Hope.
And it is the greatest infidelity.
Because it is infidelity to the greatest Faith.

Poor children, they conduct their business with wisdom during the day.

But when evening comes, they can't make up their minds,

They can't be resigned to trust my wisdom for the space of one night

With the conduct and the governing of their business.

As if I wasn't capable, if you please, of looking after it a little.

Of watching over it.

Of governing and conducting, and all that kind of stuff.

I have a great deal more business to look after, poor people, I govern creation, maybe that is more difficult.

You might perhaps, and no harm done, leave your business in my hands, O wise men.

Maybe I am just as wise as you are.

You might perhaps leave it to me for the space of a night.

While you are asleep

At last

And the next morning you might find it not too badly damaged perhaps . . .

Put off until tomorrow those tears which fill your eyes and your head,

Flooding you, rolling down your cheeks, those tears which stream down your cheeks.

Because between now and tomorrow, maybe I, God, will have passed by your way.

Human wisdom says: Woe to the man who puts off what he has to do until tomorrow.

And I say Blessed, blessed is the man who puts off what he has to do until tomorrow.

Blessed is he who puts off. That is to say Blessed is he who hopes. And who sleeps.

CHARLES PÉGUY

I. TO GOD THE FATHER

MEDITATION

Do not speak before God from knowledge, but approach Him with childish thoughts and so walk before Him that you may be blessed with the fatherly care which fathers bestow upon their children. For it is written: "The Lord preserveth the simple".

ST. ISAAK OF SYRIA · 6TH CENTURY

Even if I have gone astray, I am thy child, O God; thou art my father and mother.

ARJAN · DIED 1606 · SIKH

See note on page 284.

Thou art my father: who is my mother, who is my father? Only thou, O God.

AMERICAN-INDIAN · KEKCHI TRIBE

Most loving Lord, give me a childlike love of Thee, which may cast out all fear. Amen.

E. B. PUSEY · 1800–82

Pusey tried to find a basis for union between the Churches of England and Rome.

O God, the Father of mercies, grant unto us ever to hold fast to the spirit of adoption, whereby we cry to Thee "Father", and are called, and are, Thy sons; through Jesus Christ, our Lord. Amen.

ROMAN BREVIARY

This is the book which contains the daily service (psalms and lessons) for the four quarters of the Roman Catholic ecclesiastical year.

Thee, God, I come from, to thee go,
All day long I like fountain flow
From thy hand out, swayed about
Mote-like in thy mighty glow.

145

What I know of thee I bless,
As acknowledging thy stress
On my being and as seeing
Something of thy holiness.

Once I turned from thee and hid,
Bound on what thou hadst forbid;
Sow the wind I would; I sinned:
I repent of what I did.

Bad I am, but yet thy child.
Father, be thou reconciled,
Spare thou me, since I see
With thy might that thou art mild.

I have life before me still
And thy purpose to fulfil;
Yea a debt to pay thee yet:
Help me, sir, and so I will.

But thou bidst, and just thou art,
Me shew mercy from my heart
Towards my brother, every other
Man my mate and counterpart.

GERARD MANLEY HOPKINS

This poem was unfinished.

I have recklessly thrown aside my paternal glory, and
among the sinners I have dissipated the wealth which thou
gavest me; wherefore I cry to thee with the voice of the
Prodigal: I have sinned before thee, O Merciful Father,
receive me as a penitent, and make me as one of thy hired
servants.

EASTERN CHURCH

Bless the Lord, O my soul: and all that is within me, **bless** his holy name.

Bless the Lord, O my soul, and forget not all his benefits:

Who forgiveth all thine iniquities; who healeth all **thy** diseases;

Who redeemeth thy life from destruction; who crowneth thee with lovingkindness and tender mercies;

Who satisfieth thy mouth with good things, so that thy youth is renewed like the eagle's . . .

The Lord is merciful and gracious, slow to anger, and plenteous in mercy.

He will not always chide: neither will he keep his anger for ever . . .

Like as a father pitieth his children, so the Lord pitieth them that fear him . . .

But the mercy of the Lord is from everlasting to everlasting upon them that fear him, and his righteousness unto children's children . . .

Bless the Lord, all his works in all places of his dominion: bless the Lord, O my soul.

FROM PSALM 103

To Mercy, Pity, Peace and Love,
All pray in their distress;
And to these virtues of delight
Return their thankfulness.

For Mercy, Pity, Peace and Love
Is God, our father dear,
And Mercy, Pity, Peace, and Love
Is Man, his child and care.

For Mercy has a human heart,
Pity a human face,

And Love, the human form divine,
And Peace, the human dress.

Then every man, of every clime,
That prays in his distress,
Prays to the human form divine,
Love, Mercy, Pity, Peace.

And all must love the human form,
In heathen, turk or jew;
Where Mercy, Love, & Pity dwell
There God is dwelling too.

BLAKE

§ 2

GOD SPEAKS

My child, it is not necessary to know much to please me; it is sufficient to love much. Speak to me as thou wouldst to a father if he drew near.

Are there any for whom thou wouldst pray to me? Repeat to me the names of thy relations, thy friends; after each name add what thou wouldst have me do for them. Ask much, ask much; I love generous souls who forget themselves for others.

Tell me of the poor thou wouldst relieve, the sick whom thou hast seen suffer, the sinners thou wouldst have converted, those who are alienated from thee, whose affection thou wouldst regain.

Are there graces thou wouldst ask for thyself? Write, if thou wilt, a long list of what thou desirest, of all the needs of thy soul, and come and read it to me.

Tell me simply how proud thou art, how sensitive, egotistical, mean and indolent. Poor child, do not blush; there are in heaven many saints who had their faults; they prayed to me, and little by little their faults were corrected.

Do not hesitate to ask me for blessings for the body and mind; for health, memory and success. I can give you all things, and I always give, when my blessings are needed to render souls more holy.

Today what wilt thou have, my child? If thou knowest how I long to do thee good! Hast thou plans that occupy thee? Lay them all before me. Dost thou wish to give pleasure to thy mother, to thy family, to those on whom thou dost depend? What wouldst thou do for them?

And for me? Hast thou no zealous thought for me? Dost thou not wish to do a little good to the souls of thy friends who have perhaps forgotten me?

Bring me all thy failures, and I will show thee the cause of them. Hast thou not troubles? Who has caused thee pain? Tell me all. And wilt thou not end by adding that thou wilt pardon and forget ?—and I will bless thee.

Dost thou dread something painful? Is there in thy heart a vain fear which is not reasonable, but which is tormenting thee? Trust thyself wholly to my care. I am here. I see everything. I will not leave thee.

Hast thou not joys to be made known to me? Why dost thou not let me share thy happiness? Tell me what has happened since yesterday to cheer and console thee. An unexpected visit which did thee good; a fear suddenly dissipated; a success that thou thoughtest thou wouldst not reach; a mark of affection, a letter, 'a gift which thou hast

149

received? I have prepared it all for thee. Thou canst show thy gratitude and give me thanks.

Art thou resolved no longer to expose thyself to this temptation? not to finish this book which excites thy imagination? no longer to give thy friendship to a person who is not godly and whose presence disturbs the peace of thy soul? Wilt thou go at once to do a kindness to this companion who has hurt thee?

Well, my child, go now; take up thy work; be silent, humble, submissive and kind; and come back to-morrow, and bring me a heart still more devout and loving. To-morrow I shall have more blessings for thee.

> I cannot remember where I found the above: but I have a note that it was written by a mediaeval saint, and rendered later from the Latin by a Brahmin converted to Christianity. B.G.

MAN REPLIES

Lord, these are such little things for which we pray. If someone were to ask them of me, I could do them as well. But you are a hundred times more able than I and even more willing, so if we asked you for something greater, you could still give it—and the more willingly the greater it is that we ask for.

MEISTER ECKHART · GERMAN MYSTIC · 1260?–1327

SECOND PART

II: THY WILL BE DONE

MEDITATION

Prayer unites the soul to God. For though the soul be ever like to God in nature and substance, restored by grace, it is often unlike in condition by sin on man's part. Then is prayer a witness that the soul wills as God wills, and it comforts the conscience and enables man to grace. And so He teaches us to pray and mightily trust that we shall have it. For He beholdeth us in love and would *make us partners of His good deed*. And therefore He moves us to pray for that which it pleases Him to do.

JULIANA OF NORWICH · 14TH AND 15TH CENTURIES

Lord, we know not what is good for us. Thou knowest what it is. For it we pray.

THE KHONDS

The Khonds are an aboriginal tribe found in Orissa and the Ganjam district of Madras.

Oh Eternal Ruler, Lord of all, set in my heart the fear of thy Godhead: grant me what thou deemest best: for thou it is that hast created my life.

NEBUCHADNEZZAR

Nebuchadnezzar, King of Babylon (7th–6th century B.C.), prayed thus to Marduk on his accession. For Marduk, see note on page 283.

King Zeus, grant us the good whether we pray for it or not, but evil keep from us though we pray for it.

GREEK

Quoted by Plato in the *Alcibiades*.

O Lord, in Mercy grant my soul to live,
And patience grant, that hurt I may not grieve:
How shall I know what thing is best to seek?
Thou only knowest: what Thou knowest, give!

AL-ANSARI · DIED 1088 · SUFI

Mark me like the tulip with Thine own streaks.

JAMI · 1414–92 · SUFI

I have taken refuge in Thee. Teach me now what to do and what to say. Thy will is paramount: merge my ego in Thy Will and make me thy instrument.

RAMAKRISHNA · 1836–86 · INDIAN

The translation, we think, is by Swami Nikhalananda.

Lead me, O God, and I will follow, willingly if I am wise, but if not willingly I still must follow.

EARLY STOIC

See note on page 285.

Do with me henceforth as Thou wilt. I am of one mind with Thee, I am Thine. I decline nothing that seems good to Thee. Send me whither Thou wilt. Clothe me as Thou wilt. Will Thou that I take office or live a private life, remain at home or go into exile, be poor or rich, I will defend Thy purpose with me in respect of all these.

EPICTETUS · BORN C. A.D. 60 · STOIC

God Almighty, Eternal, Righteous, and Merciful, give to us poor sinners to do for thy sake all that we know of thy will, and to will always what pleases thee, so that inwardly purified, enlightened, and kindled by the fire of the Holy Spirit, we may follow in the footprints of thy well-beloved Son, our Lord Jesus Christ. Amen.

ST. FRANCIS OF ASSISI

Grant to us, O Lord, to know that which is worth knowing, to love that which is worth loving, to praise that which pleaseth thee most, to esteem that which is most precious unto thee, and to dislike whatsoever is evil in thy eyes. Grant us with true judgement to distinguish things that differ, and above all to search out and to do what is well pleasing unto thee, through Jesus Christ our Lord. Amen.

THOMAS à KEMPIS

God of all goodness, grant us to desire ardently, to seek wisely, to know surely, and to accomplish perfectly Thy holy will, for the glory of Thy name.

ST. THOMAS AQUINAS

O Lord Jesus Christ, Who art the Way, the Truth, and the Life, we pray Thee suffer us not to stray from Thee, who art the Way, nor to distrust Thee, who art the Truth, nor to rest in any other thing than Thee, who art the Life.

Teach us by Thy Holy Spirit what to believe, what to do, and wherein to take our rest. Amen.

ERASMUS · C. 1466–1536

Govern all by Thy wisdom, O Lord, so that my soul may always be serving Thee as Thou dost will, and not as I may choose. Do not punish me, I beseech Thee, by granting that which I wish or ask, if it offend Thy love, which would always live in me. Let me die to myself, that I may serve Thee: let me live to Thee, who in Thyself art the true Life.

ST. TERESA OF AVILA

Dispose of me according to the wisdom of thy pleasure: thy will be done, though in my own undoing.

SIR THOMAS BROWNE

Je vous ne demande ni santé, ni maladie, ni vie, ni mort, mais que vous disposiez de ma santé et de ma maladie, de ma vie et de ma mort pour votre gloire, pour mon salut et pour l'utilité de l'église et de vos saints.

PASCAL · 1623–62

Translation:

I ask of Thee neither health nor sickness, neither life nor death, but only that Thou disposest of my health and of my sickness, of my life and of my death, for Thy glory, for my salvation, and for the service of the church and Thy saints.

Herr, die Schrift sagt: "Es gibt eine Zeit zum Schweigen und eine Zeit zum Reden". Heiland, lehre mich das Schweigen aus Demut, das Schweigen aus Klugheit, das Schweigen aus Liebe, das Schweigen der Vollkommenheit, das beredte Schweigen, das Schweigen der Regeltreue.

Herr, lehre mich das Schweigen des eigenen Herzen, damit ich das Wehen des Heiligen Geistes in mir erlausche und die Tiefen Gottes erspüre.

FRANKFURT PRAYER · 16TH CENTURY

Translation:

Lord, the Scripture says: "There is a time for silence and a time for speech". Saviour, teach me the silence of humility, the silence of wisdom, the silence of love, the silence of perfection, the silence that speaks without words, the silence of faith.

Lord, teach me to silence my own heart that I may listen to the gentle movement of the Holy Spirit within me and sense the depths which are of God.

TRANSLATED BY B.G.

Father, give to Thy child that which he himself knows not how to ask. I dare not ask either for crosses or consolation; I simply present myself before Thee, I open my heart to Thee. Behold my needs which I know not myself; see and do according to Thy tender mercy. Smite or heal, depress or raise me up.

I adore all Thy purposes without knowing them.

I am silent; I offer myself in sacrifice.

I yield myself to Thee. I would have no other desire than to accomplish Thy will.

Teach me to pray.

Pray thyself in me. Amen.

FÉNELON · 1651–1715

Lord God Almighty, I charge Thee of Thy great mercy and by the token of the holy rood that Thou guide me to Thy will and to my soul's need better than I can myself, that above all things I may inwardly love Thee with a clear mind and clean body; for Thou art my Maker, my help and my hope.

KING ALFRED THE GREAT

Lord, let Thy glory be my end, Thy word my rule, and then Thy will be done.

KING CHARLES I

O merciful God, consider my misery, best known unto thee; and be thou now unto me a strong tower of defence, I humbly require thee. Suffer me not to be tempted above my power, but either be thou a deliverer unto me out of this great misery, or else give me grace patiently to bear thy heavy hand and sharp correction. It was thy right hand that delivered the people of Israel out of the hands of Pharaoh, which for the space of four hundred years did oppress them, and keep them in bondage; let it therefore likewise seem good to thy fatherly goodness, to deliver me, sorrowful wretch, for whom thy son Christ shed his precious blood on the cross, out of this miserable captivity and bondage, wherein I am now. How long wilt thou be absent?—for ever? Oh, Lord! hast thou forgotten to be gracious, and hast thou shut up thy loving kindness in displeasure? wilt thou be no more entreated? is thy mercy clear gone for ever, and thy promise come utterly to an end for evermore? why dost thou make so long tarrying? shall I despair of thy mercy? Oh God! far be that from me; I am thy workmanship, created in Christ Jesus; give me grace therefore to tarry thy leisure, and patiently to bear thy works, assuredly knowing, that as thou canst, so thou wilt deliver me, when it shall please thee, nothing doubting or mistrusting thy goodness towards me; for thou knowest better what is good for me than I do; therefore do with me in all things what thou wilt, and plague me what way thou wilt. Only, in the meantime, arm me, I beseech thee, with thy armour, that I may stand fast, my loins being girded about with verity, having on the breast-plate of righteousness, and shod with the shoes prepared by the gospel of peace; above all things, taking to me the shield of faith, wherewith I may be able to quench all the fiery darts of the wicked; and taking the helmet of salvation, and the sword of thy spirit, which is thy most holy word; praying always, with all manner of prayer and supplication, that I may refer myself wholly to thy will, abiding thy pleasure, and comforting myself in those troubles that it shall please thee to send me; seeing such troubles be profitable for me, and seeing I am assuredly persuaded that it cannot but be well all thou doest. Hear me, O merciful Father, for his sake, whom thou wouldest should be a sacrifice for my sins; to whom with thee and the Holy Ghost be all honour and glory. Amen!

LADY JANE GREY

This prayer by the girl who was Queen of England for nine days was written when she was fifteen. A year later she was executed.

III. I AND THOU

MEDITATION

God can no more do without us than we can do without Him.

MEISTER ECKHART

O this beauty of the Universe!
How did you, my Lord, come to create it?
In what outburst of ecstasy
Allowed you your Being to be manifested?
Some say you took fancy in the play of form,
Giving in delight your Absolute Being an appearance.
Dadu understands you need him
In thy play of creation.

DADU · 16TH–17TH CENTURY · HINDU

See note on page 281.

There are three different paths to reach the Highest: the path of I, the path of Thou, and the path of Thou and I.

According to the first, all that is, was, or ever shall be is I, my higher Self. In other words, I am, I was, and I shall be for ever in Eternity.

According to the second, Thou art, O Lord, and all is Thine.

And according to the third, Thou art the Lord, and I am Thy servant, or Thy son.

RAMAKRISHNA

God did not deprive thee of the operation of his love, but thou didst deprive Him of thy co-operation. God would never have rejected thee, if thou hadst not rejected his love. O all-good God, thou dost not forsake unless forsaken, thou never takest away thy gifts until we take away our hearts.

ST. FRANÇOIS DE SALES · 1567–1622

When I thus rest in the silence of contemplation, Thou, Lord, makest reply within my heart, saying: Be thou mine

and I too will be thine. . . . Thou, Lord, canst not be mine if
I be not mine own.

NICOLAS OF CUSA · BORN 1401

Thou, O God, canst never forsake me so long as I am
capable of Thee.

NICOLAS OF CUSA

What else, Lord, is Thy seeing, when Thou beholdest me
with pitying eye, than that Thou art seen of me? In beholding
me Thou givest Thyself to be seen of me, Thou who art a
hidden God. None can see Thee save in so far as Thou
grantest a sight of Thyself, nor is that sight aught else than
Thy seeing him that seeth Thee.

NICOLAS OF CUSA

For Thou art there where seeing is one with being seen,
and hearing with being heard, and tasting with being tasted,
and touching with being touched, and speaking with hearing,
and creating with speaking.

NICOLAS OF CUSA

FROM "THE HYMN OF JESUS"

I would be saved, and I would save. Amen.
I would be loosed and I would loose. Amen . . .
I would be born, and I would bear. Amen.
I would hear and I would be heard. Amen.
Grace danceth. I would pipe; dance ye all. Amen.
I would flee and I would stay. Amen.
I would adorn, and I would be adorned. Amen.
I would be united, and I would unite. Amen.

A house I have not, and I have houses. Amen.
A place I have not, and I have places. Amen.
A temple I have not, and I have temples. Amen.
A lamp am I to thee that beholdest me. Amen.
A mirror am I to thee that perceivest me. Amen.
A door am I to thee that knockest at me. Amen.
A way am I to thee a wayfarer. Amen.
Now answer thou to my dancing.

THE ACTS OF JOHN

The Acts of John is an apocryphal book of the New
Testament. See note on page 289.

This, O Lord, shows me to be equal to the angels, and
even above them, for your substance is invisible to the angels,
and your nature is inaccessible to them. Yet to me you are
wholly visible, and your substance is fused with my nature.

ST. SYMEON THE NEW THEOLOGIAN

St. Symeon (?949–1022) became Abbot of Saint-Mamas
in Constantinople.

Thou hast united, O Lord, thy divinity with our humanity
and our humanity with thy divinity, thy life with our
mortality and our mortality with thy life. Thou hast received
what was ours and given unto us what was thine.

THE SYRIAN RITE

Thou, my God, who art Love, art Love that loveth, and
Love that is loveable, and Love that is the bond between
these twain.

NICOLAS OF CUSA

O thou immortall light and heat!
Whose hand so shines through all this frame,
That by the beauty of the seat,
We plainly see, who made the same.
  Seeing thy seed abides in me,
  Dwell thou in it, and I in thee.

HENRY VAUGHAN

O God, seek me out of Thy Mercy that I may come to Thee; and draw me on with Thy Grace that I may turn to Thee.

O God, I shall never lose all hope of Thee even though I disobey Thee; and I shall never cease to fear Thee even though I obey Thee.

O God, the very worlds have themselves driven me unto Thee, and my knowledge of Thy Bounty has brought me to stand before Thee.

O God, how shall I be disappointed seeing that Thou art my hope; or how shall I be despised seeing that in Thee is my trust?

O Thou who art veiled in the shrouds of Thy Glory, so that no eye can perceive Thee! O Thou Who shinest forth in the perfection of Thy splendour, so that our hearts have realized Thy Majesty! How shalt Thou be hidden, seeing that Thou art ever Manifest: or how shalt Thou be absent, seeing that Thou art ever Present, and watchest over us?

IBN 'ATA' ALLAH · DIED 1309 · SUFI

§ 2

God in me, God beyond me! Past compare!
O Being wholly here and wholly there!

ANGELUS SILESIUS

"Angelus Silesius", who wrote largely in rhymed couplets, was the pseudonym of Johann Scheffler, a German physician (1624–77).

This also is Thou; neither is this Thou.

UNKNOWN

SECOND PART

IV. IN TEMPTATION

MEDITATION

We are told by the Psalmist first to leave evil and then to do good. I will add that if you find it difficult to follow this advice, you may first do good, and the evil will automatically depart from you.

RABBI YITZHAK MEIR OF GER · HASID

O Lord, enlighten my heart, which evil desire hath darkened ...

O Lord, grant me thought of good.

ST. JOHN CHRYSOSTOM · 345–407

O Love, no more sins! no more sins!

ST. CATHERINE OF GENOA · C. 1447–1510

I beseech Thee, O Lord, the Father, Guide of our reason, to make us mindful of the noble origin Thou hast thought worthy to confer upon us, and to assist us to act as becomes free agents, that we may be cleansed from irrational passions of the body, and may subdue and govern the same, using them as instruments in a fitting manner; and to assist us to the right direction of the reason that is in us, and to its participation in what is real by the light of truth. And thirdly, I beseech Thee, my Saviour, entirely to remove the darkness from the eyes of our souls, in order that we may know aright, as Homer says, both God and men.

SIMPLICIUS · 6TH CENTURY · NEOPLATONIST

See note on page 283.

O merciful Lord, enlighten Thou me with a clear shining inward light, and remove away all darkness from the habitation of my heart. Repress Thou my many wandering thoughts ...

THOMAS à KEMPIS

Lord, often have I thought with myself, I will sin but this one sin more, and then I will repent of it, and of all the rest of my sins together. So foolish was I and ignorant. As if I should be more able to pay my debts when I owe more; or as if I should say, I will wound my friend once again, and then I will lovingly shake hands with him: but what if my friend will not shake hands with me?

THOMAS FULLER

Lord, before I commit a sin, it seems to me so shallow that I may wade through it dry-shod from my guiltiness; but when I have committed it, it often seems so deep that I cannot escape without drowning.

THOMAS FULLER

O Lord, my God, Light of the blind and Strength of the weak; yea also, Light of those that see and Strength of the strong; hearken unto my soul, and hear it crying out of the depths.

O Lord, help us to turn and seek Thee; for Thou hast not forsaken Thy creatures as we have forsaken Thee our creator. Let us turn and seek Thee, for we know Thou art here in our hearts, when we confess to Thee, when we cast ourselves upon Thee, and weep in Thy bosom, after all our rugged ways; and Thou dost gently wipe away our tears, and we weep the more for joy; because Thou, Lord, who madest us, dost remake and comfort us.

Hear, Lord, my prayer, and grant that I may most entirely love Thee, and do Thou rescue me, O Lord, from every temptation, even unto the end. Amen.

ST. AUGUSTINE

In the hour of my distress,
When temptations me oppress,
And when I my sins confess,
    Sweet Spirit comfort me!

When I lie within my bed,
Sick in heart and sick in head,
And with doubts discomforted,
     Sweet Spirit comfort me!

When the tapers now burn blue,
And the comforters are few,
And that number more than true,
     Sweet Spirit comfort me!

When the Judgment is reveal'd,
And that open'd which was seal'd,
When to Thee I have appeal'd;
     Sweet Spirit, comfort me!

ROBERT HERRICK

§ 2

'Lead us into no such temptations, Lord!'
Yea, but O Thou whose servants are the bold,
Lead such temptations by the head and hair,
Reluctant dragons, up to who dares fight,
That so he may do battle and have praise.

ROBERT BROWNING

When the Evil Inclination whispers in my ear, let me
serve Thee *with* it.

HASIDIC

This is based on two Hasidic passages. The Evil
Inclination, in Hebrew theology, is very similar to, but
not quite identical with, Original Sin.

MEDITATION

Though a man be soiled
With the sins of a lifetime,
Let him but love me,
Rightly resolved,
In utter devotion:
I see no sinner,
That man is holy.

THE BHAGAVAD-GITA · HINDU

*The translation is by Swami Prabhavananda and
Christopher Isherwood. And see note on p 281.*

Father, I have sinned against heaven, and in Thy sight, and am no more worthy to be called Thy son.

ST. LUKE

God, be merciful to me a sinner.

ST. LUKE

O God, our sins are many; strip us of them like a garment.

A SUMERIAN POET

From a cuneiform inscription found at Akkad: about 2000 B.C.

> Lord, who has form'd me out of mud,
>   And hast redeem'd me through thy bloud,
>   And sanctifi'd me to do good;
>
> Purge all my sinnes done heretofore:
>   For I confesse my heavie score,
>   And I will strive to sinne no more.
>
> Enrich my heart, mouth, hands in me,
>   With faith, with hope, with charitie;
>   That I may runne, rise, rest with thee.

GEORGE HERBERT · 1593–1633

Guard me, O Lord, from brooding over the sin I have committed: let not my thoughts sink into the mire of my wrong-doing, but free them to offer Thee the pearl of good deeds.

If I have done much evil, grant that I may balance it by doing much good. Help me to hurry over the prayer "For my sin", and to meditate, with joy and thankfulness, on the prayer "Thou, O Lord, shalt reign".

HASIDIC

This contemporary prayer is based on old Hasidic teaching, and particularly on that of Rabbi Yitzak Meir of Ger, who died in 1866.

For thou desirest not sacrifice; else would I give it: thou delightest not in burnt offering.
The sacrifices of God are a broken spirit: a broken and a contrite heart, O God, thou wilt not despise.

FROM PSALM 51

O pitying One,
Thy pity is from the foundation of the world, and Thy Redemption
Begins already in Eternity.

BLAKE

O Lord, be gracious unto us! In all that we hear or see, in all that we say or do, be gracious unto us.
I ask pardon of the Great God. I ask pardon at the sunset, when every sinner turns to Him. Now and for ever I ask pardon of God. O Lord, cover us from our sins, guard our children and protect our weaker friends.

BEDUIN PRAYER AT SUNSET

This is a prayer of the Beduin camel-drivers.

All that we ought to have thought and have not thought;
All that we ought to have said and have not said;

All that we ought to have done and have not done;
All that we ought not to have thought and yet have thought;
All that we ought not to have spoken and yet have spoken;
All that we ought not to have done and yet have done;
For thoughts, words and works, pray we, O God, for forgive-
ness,
And repent with penance.

THE ZEND-AVESTA · ZOROASTRIAN

See note on page 286.

Forgive me my sins, O Lord; forgive me the sins of my youth and the sins of mine age, the sins of my soul and the sins of my body, my secret and my whispering sins, the sins I have done to please myself and the sins I have done to please others. Forgive those sins which I know, and the sins which I know not; forgive them, O Lord, forgive them all of Thy great goodness. Amen.

ANONYMOUS · PROBABLY 17TH CENTURY

Almighty God, Father of our Lord Jesus Christ, Maker of all things, Judge of all men; we acknowledge and bewail our manifold sins and wickedness, which we, from time to time, most grievously have committed, by thought, word and deed, against Thy Divine Majesty, provoking most justly Thy wrath and indignation against us. We do earnestly repent, and are heartily sorry for these our misdoings; the remem-brance of them is grievous upon us; the burden of them is intolerable. Have mercy upon us, have mercy upon us most merciful Father; for Thy Son our Lord Jesus Christ's sake. Forgive us all that is past; and grant that we may ever serve and please Thee in newness of life, to the honour and glory of Thy name: through Jesus Christ our Lord. Amen.

THOMAS CRANMER · 1489-1556

Lord Jesus Christ! A whole life long didst thou suffer that I too might be saved; and yet thy suffering is not yet at an end; but this too wilt thou endure, saving and redeeming me, this patient suffering of having to do with me, I who so often go astray from the right path, or even when I remained on the straight path stumbled along it or crept so slowly along the right path. Infinite patience, suffering of infinite patience. How many times have I not been impatient, wished to give up and forsake everything; wished to take the terribly easy way out, despair: but thou didst not lose patience. Oh, I cannot say what thy chosen servant says: that he filled up that which is behind of the afflictions of Christ in his flesh; no, I can only say that I increased thy sufferings, added new ones to those which thou didst once suffer in order to save me.

SÖREN KIERKEGAARD

TO THE BLESSED VIRGIN

Al myghty and al mercyable Queene,
To whom that al this world fleeth for socour
To have relees of sinne, of sorwe, and teene![1]
Glorious Virgine, of allè flourès flour,
To thee I flee confounded in errour.
Help, and releeve, thou mihti debonayre,
Have mercy on my perilous langour!
Venquisshed me hath my cruel adversaire.

Queen of comfort! yit whan I me bithinke
That I agilt[2] have bothè him and thee,
And that my soule is wurthi for to sinke,
Allas! I caitif, whider may I flee?
Who shal un-to thi Sone my menè[3] bee?
Who, but thy-self, that art of pitee welle?
Thou hast more reuthe on our adversitee
Than in this world mighte any tungè telle.

Virgine, that art so noble of apparaile,
And ledest us in-to the hyè tour
Of paradys, thou me wisse and counsaile
How I may have thy grace and thy socóur,
Al have I ben in filthe and in erróur.
Lady, un-to that court thou me ajourne
That clepéd[4] is thy bench, O freshé flour
Ther as that merci evere shal sojourne.

CHAUCER

teene = grief. [2] agilt = offended. [3] mene = mediator. [4] clepéd = called

TO GOD THE FATHER

Wilt thou forgive that sinne where I begunne,
Which is my sin, though it were done before?
Wilt thou forgive those sinnes, through which I runne,
And do run still: though still I do deplore?
    When thou hast done, thou hast not done,
        For, I have more.

Wilt thou forgive that sinne by which I' have wonne
Others to sinne? and, made my sinne their doore?
Wilt thou forgive that sinne which I did shunne
A yeare, or two: but wallowed in, a score?
    When thou hast done, thou hast not done,
        For I have more.

I have a sinne of feare, that when I have spunne
My last thred, I shall perish on the shore;
Sweare by thy selfe, that at my death thy sonne
Shall shine as he shines now, and heretofore;
    And, having done that, Thou haste done,
        I feare no more.

JOHN DONNE

FROM THE נעילה

Thou givest a hand to transgressors, and thy right hand is stretched out to receive the penitent; thou hast taught us, O Lord our God, to make confession unto thee of all our sins, in order that we may cease from the violence of our hands, that thou mayest receive us into thy presence in perfect repentance . . .

O do thou, in thy abounding compassion, have mercy upon us, for thou delightest not in the destruction of the world, as it is said, Seek ye the Lord, while he may be found, call ye upon him while he is near. And it is said, Let the wicked forsake his ways, and the man of iniquity his thoughts; and let him return unto the Lord, and he will have mercy upon him; and to our God for he will abundantly pardon. But thou art a God ready to forgive, gracious and merciful, slow to anger, plenteous in loving kindness, and abounding in goodness; thou delightest in the repentance of the wicked and hast no pleasure in their death; as it is said, Say unto them, As I live, saith the Lord God, I have no pleasure in the death of the wicked, but that the wicked turn from his way and live: turn ye, turn ye from your evil ways; for why will ye die, O house of Israel? And it is said, Have I at all any pleasure in the death of the wicked, saith the Lord God, and not rather that he should return from his way, and live? And it is said, For I have no pleasure in the death of him that dieth, saith the Lord God; therefore turn yourselves and live.

HEBREW PRAYER BOOK

The נעילה is the concluding service of the Day of Atonement. After the above prayer, which has been considerably shortened, comes the affirmation of God's Unity and the blowing of the *Shofar* or ram's horn. It was during this part of the service that the High Priest entered the Holy of Holies in the Temple and, alone there, pronounced the Ineffable Name.

190

A DIALOGUE BETWEEN GOD AND THE SOUL

Love bade me welcome: yet my soul drew back,
    Guiltie of dust and sinne.
But quick-ey'd Love, observing me grow slack
    From my first entrance in,
Drew nearer to me, sweetly questioning
    If I lack'd any thing.

'A guest,' I answer'd, 'worthy to be here':
    Love said, 'You shall be he.'
'I the unkinde, ungratefull? Ah, my deare,
    I cannot look on thee.'
Love took my hand, and smiling did reply,
    'Who made the eyes but I?'

'Truth Lord, but I have marr'd them: let my shame
    Go where it doth deserve.'
'And know you not,' sayes Love, 'who bore the blame?'
    'My deare, then I will serve.'
'You must sit down,' sayes Love, 'and taste my meat':
    So I did sit and eat.

GEORGE HERBERT

SECOND PART

VI. IN DERELICTION

MEDITATION

That man is perfect in faith who can come to God in the utter dearth of his feelings and desires, without a glow or an aspiration, with the weight of low thoughts, failures, neglects, and wandering forgetfulness, and say to Him, "Thou art my refuge".

GEORGE MACDONALD

I will love thee, O Lord, my strength . . . For thou wilt light my candle: the Lord my God will enlighten my darkness.

FROM PSALM XVIII

O my Father, if it be possible, let this cup pass from me; nevertheless not as I will, but as thou wilt.

JESUS CHRIST IN THE GARDEN

From the Gospel according to St. Matthew.

My God, my God, why hast thou forsaken me? . . . Father, into Thy hands I commend my spirit.

JESUS CHRIST ON THE CROSS

From the Gospels according to St. Matthew and St. Luke.

§ 2

How should I praise thee, Lord! how should my rymes
   Gladly engrave thy love in steel,
  If what my soul doth feel sometimes,
   My soul might ever feel!

Although there were some fourtie heav'ns, or more,
   Sometimes I peere above them all;
  Sometimes I hardly reach a score,
   Sometimes to hell I fall.

O rack me not to such a vast extent;
   Those distances belong to thee:

The world's too little for thy tent,
   A grave too big for me.

Wilt thou meet arms with man, that thou dost stretch
   A crumme of dust from heav'n to hell?
   Will great God measure with a wretch?
      Shall he thy stature spell?

O let me, when thy roof my soul hath hid,
   O let me roost and nestle there:
   Then of a sinner thou art rid,
      And I of hope and fear.

Yet take thy way; for sure thy way is best:
   Stretch or contract me thy poore debter:
   This is but tuning of my breast,
      To make the musick better.

Whether I flie with angels, fall with dust,
   Thy hands made both, and I am there:
   Thy power and love, my love and trust
      Make one place ev'ry where.

GEORGE HERBERT

         Throw away thy rod,
         Throw away thy wrath;
            O my God,
         Take the gentle path . . .

         Though I fail, I weep:
         Though I halt in pace,
            Yet I creep
         To the throne of grace.

         Then let wrath remove;
         Love will do the deed:

For with love
Stonie hearts will bleed . . .

Throw away thy rod;
Though man frailties hath,
    Thou art God:
Throw away thy wrath.

GEORGE HERBERT

Ah my deare angrie Lord,
Since thou dost love, yet strike;
Cast down, yet help afford;
Sure I will do the like.

I will complain, yet praise;
I will bewail, approve:
And all my sowre-sweet dayes
I will lament, and love.

GEORGE HERBERT

Lord! thou didst put a soul here; If I must
    Be broke again, for flints will give no fire
Without a steel, O let thy power cleer
Thy gift once more, and grind this flint to dust!

HENRY VAUGHAN

Lord, since Thou hast taken from me all that I had of
Thee, yet of Thy grace leave me the gift which every dog
has by nature: that of being true to Thee in my distress, when
I am deprived of all consolation. This I desire more fer-
vently than Thy heavenly Kingdom!

MECHTHILD OF MAGDEBURG · 13TH CENTURY

Beneath the canopy of the skies roam I night and day:
My home is in the desert by night and day.
No sickness troubleth me nor silent pain tormenteth;
One thing I know, that I sorrow night and day.

Homeless am I, O Lord: whither shall I turn?
A wanderer in the desert, whither shall I turn?
I come to Thee at last, driven from every threshold;
And if Thy door be closèd, whither shall I turn?

Blessèd are they who live in sight of Thee,
Who speak with Thee, O Lord, and dwell with Thee.
Faint are my limbs, and my heart is fearful;
Humbly I sit with those who are dear to Thee.

Drunk tho' we be with pleasure, Thou art our Faith;
Helpless, without hand or foot, Thou art our Faith;
Whether we be Nazarenes, Mussulmans or Gebres,
Whatsoe'er our creed, Thou art our Faith.

TAHIR · ? EARLY 11TH CENTURY · SUFI

The translation is by Robert Bridges and Hasan Shahid
Suhrawardy.

Good and great God, can I not think of thee,
    But it must, straight, my melancholy be?
Is it interpreted in me disease,
    That, laden with my sins, I seek for ease? . . .
As thou art all, so be thou all to me,
    First, midst, and last, converted one, and three;
My faith, my hope, my love: and in this state,
    My judge, my witness, and my advocate.
Where have I been this while exil'd from thee?
    And whither rap'd, now thou but stoop'st to me?

Dwell, dwell here still: O, being everywhere,
  How can I doubt to find thee ever, here?
I know my state, both full of shame, and scorn,
  Conceiv'd in sin, and unto labour born,
Standing with fear, and must with horror fall,
  And destin'd unto judgement, after all.

I feel my griefs too, and there scarce is ground
  Upon my flesh t'inflict another wound.
Yet dare I not complain, or wish for death
  With holy *Paul*, lest it be thought the breath
Of discontent; or that these prayers be
  For weariness of life, not love of thee.

BEN JONSON

If I could shut the gate against my thoughts
  And keep out sorrow from this room within,
Or memory could cancel all the notes
  Of my misdeeds, and I unthink my sin:
How free, how clear, how clean my soul should lie,
Discharg'd of such a loathsome company!

Or were there other rooms within my heart
  That did not to my conscience join so near,
Where I might lodge the thoughts of sin apart
  That I might not their clam'rous crying hear;
What peace, what joy, what ease should I possess,
Freed from their horrors that my soul oppress!

But, O my Saviour, who my refuge art,
  Let thy dear mercies stand 'twixt them and me,
And be the wall to separate my heart
  So that I may at length repose me free;
That peace, and joy, and rest may be within,
And I remain divided from my sin.

ANONYMOUS · 1606

Thou art my Life, my Way, my Light; in thee
I live, I move, and by thy beames I see.

Thou art my Life; if thou but turn away,
My life's a thousand deaths: thou art my Way;
Without thee, Lord, I travell not but stray.

My Light thou art; without thy glorious sight,
Mine eyes are darkned with perpetuall night.
My God, thou art my Way, my Life, my Light.

Thou art my Way; I wander, if thou fly:
Thou art my Light; If hid, how blind am I!
Thou art my Life; If thou withdraw, I die.

And yet thou turn'st away thy face, and fly'st me;
And yet I sue for grace, and thou deny'st me;
Speak, art thou angry, Lord, or only try'st me?

Disclose thy Sunbeams; close thy wings, and stay;
See, see, how I am blind, and dead, and stray,
O thou, that art my Light, my Life, my Way.

FRANCIS QUARLES · 1592-1644

Lord, make me see thy glory in every place:
If mortal beauty sets my heart aglow,
Shall not that earthly fire by thine burn low,
Extinguisht by the great light of thy grace?

Dear Lord, I cry to thee for help, O raise
Me from the misery of this blind woe,
Thy spirit alone can save me: let it flow
Through will and sense, redeeming what is base.

Thou hast given me on earth this godlike soul,
And a poor prisoner of it thou hast made
Behind weak flesh-walls; from that wretched state

How can I rescue it, how my true life find?
All goodness, Lord, must fail without thy aid:
For thou alone hast power to alter fate.

MICHELANGELO

Here am I now cast down
Beneath the black glare of a netherworld's
Dead suns, dust in my mouth, among
Dun tiers no tears refresh: am cast
Down by a lofty hand,

Hand that I love! Lord Light,
How dark is thy arm's will and ironlike
Thy ruler's finger that has sent me here!
Far from Thy face I nothing understand,
But kiss the Hand that has consigned

Me to these latter years where I must learn
The revelation of despair, and find
Among the debris of all certainties
The hardest stone on which to found
Altar and shelter for Eternity.

DAVID GASCOYNE · CONTEMPORARY

Come down, O Christ, and help me! reach Thy hand,
    For I am drowning in a stormier sea
    Than Simon on Thy Lake of Galilee:
The wine of life is spilled upon the sand,
My heart is as some famine-murdered land
    Whence all good things have perished utterly,
    And well I know my soul in Hell must lie
If I this night before God's throne should stand.

OSCAR WILDE

The poem overleaf is from *E Tenebris*, written when Wilde was a young man.

When the heart is hard and parched up, come upon me with a shower of mercy.

When grace is lost from life, come with a burst of song.

When tumultuous work raises its din on all sides shutting me out from beyond, come to me, my Lord of silence, with thy peace and rest.

When my beggarly heart sits crouched, shut up in a corner, break open the door, my king, and come with the ceremony of a king.

When desire blinds the mind with delusion and dust, O thou holy One, thou wakeful, come with thy light and thy thunder.

RABINDRANATH TAGORE

Lord, teach me to seek Thee, and reveal Thyself to me when I seek Thee. For I cannot seek Thee except Thou teach me, nor find Thee except Thou reveal Thyself. Let me seek Thee in longing, let me long for Thee in seeking: let me find Thee in love and love Thee in finding. Lord, I acknowledge and I thank Thee that Thou hast created me in this Thine image, in order that I may be mindful of Thee and love Thee: but that image has been so consumed and wasted away by vices and obscured by the smoke of wrong-doing that it cannot achieve that for which it was made, except Thou renew it and create it anew. Is the eye of the soul darkened by its infirmity, or dazzled by Thy glory? Surely, it is both darkened in itself and dazzled by Thee. Lord, this is the unapproachable light in which Thou dwellest. Truly I see it not, because it is too bright for me; and yet whatever I see, I see through it, as the weak eye sees what it sees through the light of the sun, which in the sun itself it cannot look upon. Oh supreme and unapproachable light, oh holy and blessed truth, how far art Thou from me who am so near to Thee, how far art Thou removed from my vision, though I am so near to Thine! Everywhere Thou art wholly present, and I see Thee not. In Thee I move and in Thee I have my being, and cannot come to Thee; Thou art within me and about me, and I feel Thee not.

ST. ANSELM · 1033?–1109

O All-seeing Light, and eternal Life of all things, to whom nothing is either so great that it may resist, or so small that it is contemned; look upon my misery with Thine eye of mercy, and let Thine infinite power vouchsafe to limit out some proportion of deliverance unto me, as to Thee shall seem most convenient. Let not injury, O Lord, triumph over me, and let my faults by Thy hand be corrected, and make not mine enemy the minister of Thy justice. But yet, O Lord, if, in Thy wisdom, this be the aptest chastisement for my inexcusable folly; if this low bondage be fittest for my over-high desires; and the pride of my not enough humble heart be thus to be broken, O Lord, I yield unto Thy will, and joyfully embrace what sorrow thou wilt have me suffer. Only this let me crave of Thee ... that Thou wilt suffer some beams of Thy majesty to shine into my mind, that it may still depend confidently on Thee. Let calamity be the exercise, but not the overthrow of my virtue: let their power prevail, but prevail not to destruction ... But, O Lord, let never their wickedness have such a hand, but that I may carry a pure mind in a pure body.

SIR PHILIP SIDNEY

Charles I copied out this prayer for his own use.

O Domine Deus, speravi in te!
O care mi Jesu, nunc libera me!

In dura catena, in misera poena,
Languendo, gemendo, et genu flectendo,
Adoro, imploro, ut liberes me!

MARY QUEEN OF SCOTS

Translation:

O Lord my God, I have hoped in Thee,
Jesus beloved, now set me free.
In harshest chain, in wretched pain,
In weakness and in sorrow sair,
Upon my knees and at my prayer,
I beg Thee that Thou freeest me.

TRANSLATED BY B.G.

This is thought to have been written a little while
before her execution.

Show Thy mercy to me, O Lord, to glad my heart withal.
Lo, here the man that was caught of thieves, wounded, and
left for half-dead, as he was going towards Jericho. Thou
kind-hearted Samaritan, take me up . . . Deal favourably with
me according to Thy good pleasure, that I may dwell in Thy
house all the days of my life, and praise Thee for ever and
ever with them that are there.

ST. JEROME · C. 340–420

§ 4

Bestow, O God, this grace on us, that in the school of
suffering we may learn self-conquest, and through sorrow,
even if it be against our will, learn self-control.

ADAPTED FROM AESCHYLUS

O Gott, gib mir Kraft, mich zu besiegen, mich darf ja
nichts ans Leben fesseln. O leite meinen Geist, o hebe mich
aus dieser schweren Tiefe, durch deine Kunst entzückt, damit
ich furchtlos strebe aufwärts in feurigen Schwung. Denn du,
du weisst allein, du kannst allein mich begeistern.

BEETHOVEN

Translation:

O God give me strength to be victorious over myself, for
nothing may chain me to this life. O guide my spirit, O raise
me from these dark depths, that my soul, transported through
Thy wisdom, may fearlessly struggle upward in fiery flight.
For Thou alone understandest and canst inspire me.

This was written by Beethoven when he realized that
his deafness was incurable.

Look down, Great Master of the feast; O shine,
And turn once more our water into wine!

HENRY VAUGHAN

There follows a Coda
to this group
of prayers in dereliction:
prayers on recovery from dereliction

I strove towards thee, and was repulsed by thee that I might taste death. The disturbed and darkened vision of my mind was being healed from day to day by the keen salve of wholesome pains. I became more wretched, and thou nearer.

ST. AUGUSTINE

O Lord, my God! the amazing horrors of darkness were gathered round me, and covered me all over, and I saw no way to go forth; I felt the depth and extent of the misery of my fellow-creatures separated from the Divine harmony, and it was heavier than I could bear, and I was crushed down under it; I lifted up my hand, I stretched out my arm, but there was none to help me; I looked round about and was amazed. In the depths of misery, O Lord, I remembered that Thou art omnipotent; that I had called Thee Father; and I felt that I loved Thee, and I was made quiet in my will, and I waited for deliverance from Thee. Thou hadst pity upon me, when no man could help me; I saw that meekness under suffering was shown to us in the most affecting example of Thy son, and Thou taughtest me to follow Him, and I said, "Thy will, O Father, be done!"

JOHN WOOLMAN

John Woolman (1720–72) was an American Quaker who devoted his life to witness against slavery.

THE FLOWER

How fresh, O Lord, how sweet and clean
Are thy returns! ev'n as the flowers in Spring,
To which, besides their own demean,
The late-past frosts tributes of pleasure bring;
Grief melts away
Like snow in May,
As if there were no such cold thing.

Who would have thought my shrivel'd heart
Could have recover'd greennesse? It was gone
   Quite under ground; as flow'rs depart
To see their mother-root, when they have blown;
       Where they together
       All the hard weather,
Dead to the world, keep house unknown.

   These are thy wonders, Lord of power,
Killing and quickning, bringing down to hell
   And up to heaven in an houre;
Making a chiming of a passing-bell.
       We say amisse
       This or that is;
Thy word is all, if we could spell.

   O that I once past changing were,
Fast in thy Paradise, where no flower can wither!
   Many a Spring I shoot up fair,
Offring at Heav'n, growing and groning thither;
       Nor doth my flower
       Want a spring-showre,
My sinnes and I joining together.

   But while I grow in a straight line,
Still upwards bent, as if Heav'n were mine own,
   Thy anger comes, and I decline:
What frost to that? what pole is not the zone,
       Where all things burn,
       When thou dost turn,
And the least frown of Thine is shown?

   And now in age I bud again,
After so many deaths I live and write;
   I once more smell the dew and rain,
And relish versing: O, my onely Light,

It cannot be
That I am he
On whom thy tempests fell all night.

These are thy wonders, Lord of love,
To make us see we are but flow'rs that glide;
Which when we once can finde and prove,
Thou hast a garden for us where to bide;
Who would be more,
Swelling through store,
Forfeit their Paradise by their pride.

GEORGE HERBERT

VII. AT THE CONTEMPLATION OF DEATH

MEDITATION

Things cannot get out of their natures, or be or not be in despite of their constitutions. Rational existences in Heaven perish not at all, and but partially on Earth: that which is thus once will in some way be always: the first Living human Soul is still alive, and all Adam hath found no Period.

SIR THOMAS BROWNE

Eternal and most glorious God, suffer me not so to under-value myself as to give away my soul, Thy soul, Thy dear and precious soul, for nothing; and all the world is nothing, if the soul must be given for it. Preserve therefore my soul, O Lord, because it belongs to Thee, and preserve my body because it belongs to my soul. Thou alone dost steer my boat through all its voyage, but hast a more special care of it, when it comes to a narrow current, or to a dangerous fall of waters. Thou hast a care of the preservation of my body in all the ways of my life; but, in the straits of death, open Thine eyes wider, and enlarge Thy Providence towards me so far that no illness or agony may shake and benumb the soul. Do Thou so make my bed in all my sickness that, being used to Thy hand, I may be content with any bed of Thy making. Amen.

JOHN DONNE (ADAPTED)

O Christ, when I at last my arms lay down
Bring me, Thy soldier, to Thy blessed town,
O Thou, that art the soldier's palm and crown.
The battle knows no end; give me Thy power;
Deny me not Thy peace, when comes my hour;
Deny me not Thyself, the eternal dower.

ST. PIETRO DAMIANI · 1007–72

St. Pietro Damiani, sometime Cardinal Bishop of Ostia, was a prominent ecclesiastical reformer.

The Divine Vision still was seen,
Still was the Human Form Divine,
Weeping in weak & mortal clay,
O Jesus, still the Form was thine.

And thine the Human Face, & thine
The Human Hands & Feet & Breath,

Entering thro' the Gates of Birth
And passing thro' the Gates of Death.

BLAKE

Before the beginning Thou hast foreknown the end,
  Before the birthday the death-bed was seen of Thee:
Cleanse what I cannot cleanse, mend what I cannot mend,
  O Lord All-Merciful, be merciful to me.

While the end is drawing near I know not mine end;
  Birth I recall not, my death I cannot foresee:
O God, arise to defend, arise to befriend,
  O Lord All-Merciful, be merciful to me.

CHRISTINA ROSSETTI

Even such is Time, which takes in trust
  Our youth, our joys, and all we have,
And pays us but with age and dust:
  Who in the dark and silent grave,
When we have wandered all our ways
  Shuts up the story of our days:
And from which earth and grave and dust,
The Lord shall raise me up, I trust.

SIR WALTER RALEIGH

These lines are said to have been found between the
pages of his Bible, having been written, it is surmised,
a few hours before his execution.

O God within my breast,
Almighty, ever-present Deity!

Life—that in me has rest
As I—undying Life—have power in Thee.

Vain are the thousand creeds
That move men's hearts, unutterably vain,
Worthless as withered weeds,
Or idle froth amid the boundless main,

To waken doubt in one
Holding so fast by Thine infinity;
So surely anchored on
The steadfast rock of immortality.

With wide-embracing love
Thy spirit animates eternal years,
Pervades and broods above,
Changes, sustains, dissolves, creates and rears.

Though Earth and moon were gone
And suns and universes ceased to be
And Thou wert left alone
Every Existence would exist in Thee.

There is not room for Death,
Nor atom that his might could render void:
Thou—Thou art Being and Breath,
And what Thou art may never be destroyed.

EMILY BRONTË · 1818–48

Thou in me and I in thee. Death! what is death? There is no
death: *in thee* it is impossible, absurd.

MARK RUTHERFORD · 1829–1913

Lord, grant that my last hour may be my best hour.

John Aubrey, antiquarian and author of *Brief Lives*
(1626–97), records this prayer as one that "was wont
to be said, by ancient people, before the Civil Wars".

To have given me self-consciousness but for an hour in a
world so breathless with beauty would have been enough.
But thou hast preserved it within me for twenty years now
and more, and hast crowned it with the joy of this summer
of summers. And so come what may, whether life or death,
and, if death, whether bliss unimaginable or nothingness, I
thank thee and bless thy name.

This was written a few days after the outbreak of the first
world war by a friend who was at Oxford with me from
1912 to 1914, and was killed in 1917. The summer of
1914 was exceptionally beautiful, or seemed so to us as
we slept "out" under the old City wall, or walked in the
New College garden, or lay reading in a punt on the
river.   V.G.

§ 2

Deathbed Confession:

I acknowledge unto thee, O Lord my God and God of
my fathers, that both my cure and my death are in thy hands.
May it be thy will to send me a perfect healing. Yet if my
death be fully determined by thee, I will in love accept it at
thy hand . . .

Thou who art the father of the fatherless and judge of the
widow, protect my beloved kindred with whose soul my own is
knit. Into thy hand I commend my spirit . . . Amen, and Amen!

Last words of the above, when death is imminent:

The Lord reigneth; the Lord hath reigned; the Lord shall reign for ever and ever.

Blessed be His name, whose glorious kingdom is for ever and ever.

The Lord, He is God.

Hear O Israel, the Lord our God, the Lord is One.

THE HEBREW PRAYER BOOK

Gandhi's last words, after his assassination:

He, Ram! He, Ram! (Ah, God! Ah, God!)

THIRD PART

I. "SO PANTETH MY SOUL AFTER THEE, O GOD"

MEDITATION

The desire and pursuit of the whole is called love.

PLATO

Too late came I to love thee, O thou Beauty both so
ancient and so fresh, yea too late came I to love thee. And
behold, thou wert within me, and I out of myself, where I
made search for thee: I ugly rushed headlong upon those
beautiful things thou hast made. Thou indeed wert with me;
but I was not with thee: these beauties kept me far enough
from thee: even those, which unless they were in thee, would
not be at all. Thou calledst and criedst unto me, yea thou
even breakedst open my deafness: thou discoveredst thy
beams and shinedst unto me, and didst cast away my
blindness: thou didst most fragrantly blow upon me, and I
drew in my breath and I panted after thee; I tasted thee,
and now do hunger and thirst after thee; thou didst touch
me, and I ever burn again to enjoy thy peace.

ST. AUGUSTINE

O Lord our God, grant us grace to desire thee with our
whole heart; that, so desiring, we may seek, and, seeking, find
thee; and so finding thee, may love thee; and loving thee,
may hate those sins from which thou hast redeemed. Amen.

ST. ANSELM

O God, give me faith, devotion and love,
So that I may constantly chant Thy Holy name.
Let my heart overflow with Thy love.
Let me realize what ravishment is there in Thy name,
And let my being be firmly rooted in Thee.
Thou are the indwelling Spirit: awaken my soul;
Let my soul be in holy communion with Thee,
    And let that communion be constant.
    Then, O merciful God, Thy supreme light will ever
shine in my life.

DADU

Let me behold thy Godhead, let me attain my heart's desire: set righteousness on my lips and grace in my heart.

PRAYER TO MARDUK · BABYLONIAN

See note on page 283.

Adoring thy goodness, we make this our only prayer . . . that thou wouldst be willing to keep us all our lives in the love of thy knowledge.

ATTRIBUTED TO APULEIUS

This prayer, attributed to the Platonic philosopher and author of the *Golden Ass* (born about A.D. 125), is addressed to Asklepios, God of Healing.

O Lord, give me understanding concerning Thyself, for I cannot understand Thee except by means of Thee.

ABU YAZID · 9TH CENTURY · SUFI

O God! if I worship Thee in fear of Hell, burn me in Hell; and if I worship Thee in hope of Paradise, exclude me from Paradise; but if I worship Thee for Thine own sake, withhold not Thine Everlasting Beauty!

RABI'A · DIED 801 · SUFI

My Lord and God. I do not desire Thy Paradise; I do not desire the bliss of the After World; I desire only Thee Thyself.

THE RABBI OF LADI · DIED 1813 · HASID

Whatever share of this world Thou dost bestow on me, bestow it on Thine enemies, and whatever share of the next world thou dost give me, give it to Thy friends. Thou art enough for me!

RABI'A

O God, Thou knowest that Paradise weighs with me not so much as the wing of a gnat beside the honour which Thou hast done unto me, and beside Thy love and Thy giving me intimacy with the praise of Thy name, and beside the peace of mind which Thou hast given me when I meditate on Thy Majesty. If Thou befriendest me by Thy recollection, and sustainest me with Thy love, and makest it easy for me to obey Thee, then give Thou Paradise to whomsoever Thou wilt.

IBRAHIM b. ADHAM · 8TH CENTURY · SUFI

According to legend Ibrahim was a prince of Balkh, who one day suddenly cast off his royal robes and became a wandering Sufi. The above is a combination of two prayers.

O Lord, I, a beggar, ask of Thee more than a thousand kings may ask of Thee. Each one has something he needs to ask of Thee; I have come to ask Thee to give me Thyself.

AL-ANSARI · SUFI

Here is Thy virtue, here is Thy vice. Take them both and grant me only pure love for Thee. Here is Thy knowledge, here is Thy ignorance. Take them both and grant me only pure love for Thee. Here is Thy purity, here is Thy impurity. Take them both, and grant me only pure love for Thee.

RAMAKRISHNA

Lord of Creation! I do not know how to pray; I do not know what to say—I give Thee the entire prayer book.

HASIDIC

It is related that a little farmer boy, having been left an orphan at an early age, was unable to read, but had inherited a large, heavy prayer book from his parents: and that one Day of Atonement he brought it into the synagogue, laid it on the reading-desk, and, weeping, cried out as above.

I asked for Peace—
My sins arose,
And bound me close,
I could not find release.

I asked for Truth—
My doubts came in,
And with their din
They wearied all my youth.

I asked for Love—
My lovers failed,
And griefs assailed
Around, beneath, above.

I asked for Thee—
And Thou didst come
To take me home
Within Thy heart to be.

D. M. DOLBEN · 1848–77

This young poet, drowned at Oxford, was a contemporary of Robert Bridges, who greatly respected him, as did Gerard Manley Hopkins.

What pearl art Thou, that no man may pay the price?
What doth the World offer, which is not a gift from Thee?
What punishment is greater, than to dwell afar from thy
    Face?
Torture not thy slave, tho' he be unworthy of Thee!

Whoever is whelm'd in the waves of Chance, can never
    escape, if he look not to Thee as Friend.
The World hath no permanence: what it hath I esteem as
    perishable, for it is strange to thy permanence. . . .
My wish ever is to fling my heart and my soul at thy Feet.
Dust be on the head of the soul, that hath received not the
    dust of thy Feet! . . .
I will not shun thy stroke: for impure is the heart that hath
    not burned in the flame of thine Affliction.
No end is there, O Lord, to thy praises and no count of thy
    Praisers.
What atom is there that danceth not with abandon in thy
    praise?

Shams-i-Tabriz, beauty and pride of the skies, saith:
What king is there, but with heart and soul is a beggar of Thee?

JALALU D-DIN RUMI · 1207-73 · SUFI

The translation is by Robert Bridges and Hasan Shahid
Suhrawardy.

Never weather-beaten sail more willing bent to shore,
Never tired pilgrim's limbs affected slumber more,
Than my wearied sprite now longs to fly out of my troubled
    breast:
O come quickly, sweetest Lord, and take my soul to rest!

Ever blooming are the joys of heaven's high Paradise,
Cold age deafs not there our ears nor vapour dims our eyes:

233

Glory there the sun outshines; whose beams the Blessèd
   only see:
O come quickly, glorious Lord, and raise my sprite to Thee!

THOMAS CAMPION · 1567–1620

God has really favoured me: my doubts and delirium are
at an end. God and self are now lying on the same couch
in me. . . .

If I mean to worship Thee, such worship becomes impossible, as Thou art identical with all means of worship. Tell
me, O God, how I may worship Thee. If I may give Thee
ablution of water, Thou art that Thyself. Thou art the scent
of scents, and the fragrance of flowers. If I am to sing a song,
Thou art that song. If I sound the cymbals, Thou art those.
There is no place whereon I could now dance. The whole
world is filled by Thee.

TUKARAM · 1608–49 · HINDU

Werd als ein Kind, werd taub und blind
Dein eignes Icht muss werden nicht.
All Icht, all Nicht treib ferne nur;
Lass Statt, lass Zeit, auch Bald lass weit,
Geh ohne Weg den schmalen Steg,
So kommst Du auf der Wüste Spur.
O Seele mein, aus Gott geh ein,
Sink als ein Icht in Gottes Nicht.
Sink in die ungegründte Flut.
Flieh ich von Dir, Du kommst zu mir.
Verlass ich mich, so find ich Dich.
O überwesentliches Gut!

ANONYMOUS · 13TH CENTURY

Translation:

Be as a child; be deaf, be blind, for thine own self must cease to be. Leave place, leave time and images, and wander down the pathless way until you find the wilderness.

O my soul, go out from God till you sink your I into the nothingness of God, till you sink into the measureless flood.

If I flee from Thee, Thou comest to me. If I leave myself, then I find Thee, O goodness supreme.

TRANSLATED BY B.G.

Thou sweet Well for him who thirsteth in the desert! It is closed to him who speaks, but it is open to him who is silent. When he who is silent comes, lo, he finds the Well.

EGYPTIAN · 1300TH CENTURY B.C.

The translation is by Professor J. H. Breasted.

God be in my head
And in my understanding;
God be in myne eyes,
And in my looking;
God be in my mouth,
And in my speaking;
God be in my heart,
And in my thynking;
God be at my end,
And at my departing.

SARUM MISSAL

THIRD PART

II. WORSHIP, THANKSGIVING AND JOY

MEDITATION

I place before my inward eyes myself with all that I am—
my body, soul, and all my powers—and I gather round me
all the creatures which God ever created in heaven, on earth,
and in all the elements, each one severally with its name,
whether birds of the air, beasts of the forest, fishes of the
water, leaves and grass of the earth, or the innumerable
sand of the sea, and to these I add all the little specks of
dust which glance in the sunbeams, with all the little drops
of water which ever fell or are falling from dew, snow, or
rain, and I wish that each of these had a sweetly sounding
stringed instrument, fashioned from my heart's inmost
blood, striking on which they might each send up to our dear
and gentle God a new and lofty strain of praise for ever and
ever. And then the loving arms of my soul stretch out and
extend themselves towards the innumerable multitude of
all creatures, and my intention is, just as a free and blithe-
some leader of a choir stirs up the singers of his company,
even so to turn them all to good account by inciting them
to sing joyously, and to offer up their hearts to God.
"Sursum corda."

HEINRICH SUSO · GERMAN MYSTIC · C. 1300–66

§ 1

Now we must praise the author of the heavenly kingdom,
the Creator's power and counsel, the deeds of the Father of
glory; how he, the eternal God, was the author of all marvels
—He, who first gave to the sons of men the heaven for a roof,
and then, Almighty Guardian of mankind, created the earth.

CAEDMON · FLORUIT 685

This is translated from the Northumbrian language in
which Caedmon wrote.

Who then may sing Thy praise of Thee or to Thee?
Whither am I to turn my eyes to sing Thy praise? above,
below, within, without? . . . All are in Thee; all are from
Thee, O Thou who givest all and takest nought, for Thou
hast all and nought is there Thou hast not.

EGYPTIAN · C. 350 B.C.

The translation is by Professor J. H. Breasted, with
slight modifications.

What else can I do, a lame old man, but sing hymns to
God? If I were a nightingale, I would do the nightingale's
part; if I were a swan, I would do as a swan. But now I am
a rational creature, and I ought to praise God: this is my work;
I do it, nor will I desert my post, so long as I am allowed to
keep it. And I exhort you to join me in this same song.

EPICTETUS · GREEK STOIC

Lord of fire and death, of wind and moon and waters,
Father of the born, and this world's father's Father.
Hail, all hail to you—a thousand salutations.

Take our salutations, Lord, from every quarter,
Infinite of might and boundless in your glory,
You are all that is, since everywhere we find you . . .

Author of this world, the unmoved and the moving,
You alone are fit for worship, you the highest.
Where in the three worlds shall any find your equal?

Therefore I bow down, prostrate and ask for pardon:
Now forgive me, God, as friend forgives his comrade,
Father forgives son, and man his dearest lover.

THE BHAGAVAD-GITA · HINDU

The translation is by Swami Prabhavananda and Christopher Isherwood.

God is in the water, God is in the dry land, God is in the heart.
God is in the forest, God is in the mountain, God is in the cave.
God is in the earth, God is in heaven . . .
Thou art in the tree, thou art in its leaves,
Thou art in the earth, thou art in the firmament.

GOVIND SINGH · SIKH

Hast thou not seen how all in the Heavens and in the Earth uttereth the praise of God?—the very birds as they spread their wings? Every creature knoweth its prayer and its praise! and God knoweth what they do.

THE KORAN

We praise thee, O God: we acknowledge Thee to be the Lord.
All the earth doth worship Thee: the Father everlasting.

To Thee all angels cry aloud: the Heavens and all the Powers
   therein.
To Thee Cherubin and Seraphin: continually do cry,
Holy, Holy, Holy, Lord God of Sabaoth;
Heaven and earth are full of the Majesty: of Thy glory.
The glorious company of the Apostles: praise Thee.
The goodly fellowship of the Prophets: praise Thee.
The noble army of Martyrs: praise Thee.
The holy Church throughout all the world: doth acknow-
   ledge Thee . . .
Day by day: we magnify Thee;
And we worship Thy name: ever world without end. Amen.

CHRISTIAN TE DEUM

Perhaps written by Nicetas, Bishop of Remesiana,
about 410.

Praise the Lord! ye heavens, adore him;
Praise him, Angels, in the height;
Sun and moon, rejoice before him,
Praise him, all ye stars and light:
Praise the Lord! for he hath spoken,
Worlds his mighty voice obeyed;
Laws, which never shall be broken,
For their guidance hath he made.

Praise the Lord! for he is glorious;
Never shall his promise fail;
God hath made his Saints victorious,
Sin and death shall not prevail.
Praise the God of our salvation;
Hosts on high, his power proclaim;
Heaven and earth, and all creation,
Laud and magnify his name.

HYMN OF THE FOUNDLING HOSPITAL · 1796

The London Foundling Hospital was famous for its collection of beautiful hymns, and for its musical service. Handel frequently had "The Messiah" performed there.

Bless the Lord, O my soul. O Lord my God, thou art very great; thou art clothed with honour and majesty.

Who coverest thyself with light as with a garment: who stretchest out the heavens like a curtain:

Who layeth the beams of his chambers in the waters: who maketh the clouds his chariot: who walketh upon the wings of the wind:

Who maketh his angels spirits; his ministers a flaming fire. . . .

He sendeth the springs into the valleys, which run among the hills.

They give drink to every beast of the field: the wild asses quench their thirst.

By them shall the fowls of the heaven have their habitation, which sing among the branches.

He watereth the hills from his chambers: the earth is satisfied with the fruit of thy works.

He causeth the grass to grow for the cattle, and herb for the service of man: that he may bring forth food out of the earth

And wine that maketh glad the heart of man, and oil to make his face to shine, and bread which strengtheneth man's heart

The trees of the Lord are full of sap; the cedars of Lebanon, which he hath planted;

Where the birds make their nests: as for the stork, the fir trees are her house.

The high hills are a refuge for the wild goats; and the rocks for the conies.

He appointed the moon for seasons: the sun knoweth his going down.

Thou makest darkness, and it is night: wherein all the beasts of the forest do creep forth. . . .

Man goeth forth unto his work and to his labour until the evening.

O Lord, how manifold are thy works! in wisdom hast thou made them all: the earth is full of thy riches.

So is this great and wide sea, wherein are things creeping innumerable, both small and great beasts.

There go the ships: there is that leviathan, whom thou hast made to play therein.

These wait all upon thee; that thou mayest give them their meat in due season.

That thou givest them they gather: thou openest thine hand, they are filled with good. . . .

Thou sendest forth thy spirit, they are created: and thou renewest the face of the earth.

The glory of the Lord shall endure for ever: the Lord shall rejoice in his works. . . .

FROM PSALM 104

Praise ye the Lord. Praise ye the Lord from the heavens: praise him in the heights.

Praise ye him, all his angels; praise ye him, all his hosts.

Praise ye him, sun and moon: praise him, all ye stars of light.

Praise him, ye heavens of heavens and ye waters that be above the heavens.

Let them praise the name of the Lord: for he commanded, and they were created.

He hath also stablished them for ever and ever: he hath made a decree which shall not pass.

Praise the Lord from the earth, ye dragons and all deeps:

Fire, and hail; snow, and vapours; stormy wind fulfilling his word:

Mountains, and all hills: fruitful trees and all cedars:

Beasts, and all cattle; creeping things, and flying fowl:

Kings of the earth, and all people; princes, and all judges of the earth;

Both young men, and maidens; old men, and children:
Let them praise the name of the Lord: for his name alone i
  excellent; and his glory is above the earth and heaven...

PSALM 148

All cattle rest upon their pasturage,
The trees and the plants flourish,
The birds flutter in their marshes,
Their wings uplifted in adoration to thee.
All the sheep dance upon their feet,
All winged things fly,
They live when thou hast shone upon them.
The barques sail up-stream and down-stream alike.
Every highway is open because thou dawnest.
The fish in the river leap up before thee.
Thy rays are in the midst of the great green sea.

Creator of the germ in woman,
Maker of seed in man,
Giving life to the son in the body of his mother,
Soothing him that he may not weep,
Nurse (even) in the womb,
Giver of breath to animate every one that he maketh!
When he cometh forth from the womb ... on the day
  of his birth,
Thou openest his mouth in speech,
Thou suppliest his necessities.
When the fledgling in the egg chirps in the shell
Thou givest him breath therein to preserve him
  alive ...

He goeth about upon his two feet
When he hath come forth therefrom.
How manifold are thy works!
They are hidden from before (us)

O sole God, whose powers no other possesseth.
Thou didst create the earth according to thy heart

While thou wast alone:
Men, all cattle, large and small,
All that are upon the earth,
That go about upon their feet;
(All) that are on high
That fly with their wings.
The foreign countries, Syria and Kush,
The land of Egypt,
Thou settest every man into his place,
Thou suppliest their necessities . . .

FROM THE HYMN TO ATON

This is from the translation by Professor J. H. Breasted
in the *Encyclopaedia Britannica*. The hymn is probably
by Ikhnaton, who came to the throne of Egypt (as
Amenhotep IV) about 1375 B.C., and established Aton,
the Sun, as the one true God, the one loving Father of
all peoples. Professor Breasted describes him as the
earliest monotheist, universalist and idealist, and points
out the identity of the general arrangement in this
Hymn with that in Psalm CIV, many centuries later.
It is to be noted, too, that the "foreign countries",
Syria and Kush, are put before Egypt, just as Isaiah
writes, also many centuries later, "In that day shall
Israel be the third with Egypt and with Assyria, even a
blessing in the midst of the land: Whom the Lord of
hosts shall bless, saying, Blessed be Egypt my people,
and Assyria the work of my hands, and Israel my inheritance".

Most High, Omnipotent, Good Lord.
Thine be the praise, the glory, the honour, and all benediction.
To Thee alone, Most High, they are due,
    and no man is worthy to mention Thee.

Be Thou praised, my Lord, with all Thy creatures,
  above all Brother Sun,
  who gives the day and lightens us therewith.

And he is beautiful and radiant with great splendour,
  of Thee, Most High, he bears similitude.

Be Thou praised, my Lord, of Sister Moon and the stars,
  in the heaven hast Thou formed them, clear and precious
    and comely . . .

Be Thou praised, my Lord, of Sister Water,
  which is much useful and humble and precious and pure.

Be Thou praised, my Lord, of Brother Fire,
  by which Thou hast lightened the night,
  and he is beautiful and joyful and robust and strong.

Be Thou praised, my Lord, of our Sister Mother Earth,
  which sustains and hath us in rule,
  and produces divers fruits with coloured flowers and
    herbs. . . .

Praise ye and bless my Lord, and give Him thanks,
  and serve Him with great humility.

THE MIRROR OF PERFECTION · FRANCISCAN

Dance, my heart! dance to-day with joy.
The strains of love fill the days and the nights with music,
  and the world is listening to its melodies:
Mad with joy, life and death dance to the rhythm of this
  music. The hills and the sea and the earth dance. The
  world of man dances in laughter and tears.
Why put on the robe of the monk, and live aloof from the
  world in lonely pride?

Behold! my heart danceth in the delight of a hundred arts;
and the Creator is well pleased.

KABIR · 15TH CENTURY

Kabir, the weaver mystic of Northern India, is claimed
both by Hindus and by Muslims. The translation is by
Tagore.

Shall I, a gnat which dances in Thy ray,
Dare to be reverent?

COVENTRY PATMORE

We praise Thee, O God, for Thy glory displayed in all the
creatures of the earth,
In the snow, in the rain, in the wind, in the storm; in all of
Thy creatures, both the hunters and the hunted.
For all things exist only as seen by Thee, only as known by
Thee, all things exist
Only in Thy light, and Thy glory is declared even in that
which denies Thee; the darkness declares the glory of
light.
Those who deny Thee could not deny, if Thou didst not
exist; and their denial is never complete, for if it were
so, they would not exist.
They affirm Thee in living; all things affirm Thee in living;
the bird in the air, both the hawk and the finch; the
beast on the earth, both the wolf and the lamb; the
worm in the soil and the worm in the belly.
Therefore man, whom Thou hast made to be conscious of
Thee, must consciously praise Thee, in thought and in
word and in deed.
Even with the hand to the broom, the back bent in laying
the fire, the knee bent in cleaning the hearth, we,
the scrubbers and sweepers of Canterbury,

The back bent under toil, the knee bent under sin, the hands
    to the face under fear, the head bent under grief,
Even in us the voices of seasons, the snuffle of winter, the
    song of spring, the drone of summer, the voices of
    beasts and of birds, praise Thee.
We thank Thee for Thy mercies of blood, for Thy redemption
    by blood. For the blood of Thy martyrs and saints
Shall enrich the earth, shall create the holy places.
For wherever a saint has dwelt, wherever a martyr has given
    his blood for the blood of Christ,
There is holy ground, and the sanctity shall not depart from it
Though armies trample over it, though sightseers come with
    guide-books looking over it;
From where the western seas gnaw at the coast of Iona,
To the death in the desert, the prayer in forgotten places by
    the broken imperial column,
From such ground springs that which forever renews the
    earth
Though it is forever denied. Therefore, O God, we thank
    Thee
Who hast given such blessing to Canterbury.

Forgive us, O Lord, we acknowledge ourselves as type of the
    common man,
Of the men and women who shut the door and sit by the
    fire;
Who fear the blessing of God, the loneliness of the night of
    God, the surrender required, the deprivation inflicted;
Who fear the injustice of men less than the justice of God;
Who fear the hand at the window, the fire in the thatch, the
    fist in the tavern, the push into the canal,
Less than we fear the love of God.
We acknowledge our trespass, our weakness, our fault; we
    acknowledge
That the sin of the world is upon our heads; that the blood
    of the martyrs and the agony of the saints

Is upon our heads.
Lord, have mercy upon us.
Christ, have mercy upon us.
Lord, have mercy upon us.
Blessed Thomas, pray for us.

T. S. ELIOT

From *Murder in the Cathedral*.

§ 2

It is Thou who givest the bright sun, together with the ice;
it is Thou who createdst the rivers and the salmon in the river.

That the nut-tree should be flowering, O Christ, it is a
rare craft; through Thy skill too comes the kernel, Thou fair
ear of our wheat.

Though the children of Eve ill deserve the bird-flocks and
the salmon, it was the Immortal One on the cross who made
both the salmon and birds.

It is He who makes the flower of the sloe grow through
the bark of the blackthorn, and the nut-flower on the trees;
beside this, what miracle is greater?

TADHG ÓG Ó HUIGINN

He was an Irish poet, 16th century.

O world, I cannot hold thee close enough!
   Thy winds, thy wide grey skies!
   Thy mists that roll and rise!
Thy woods, this autumn day, that ache and sag
And all but cry with color! That gaunt crag
To crush! To lift the lean of that black bluff!
World, world, I cannot get thee close enough!

Long have I known a glory in it all,
   But never knew I this;
   Here such a passion is
As stretcheth me apart. Lord I do fear
Thou'st made the world too beautiful this year.
My soul is all but out of me,—let fall
No burning leaf; prithee, let no bird call.

EDNA ST. VINCENT MILLAY

She was an American poet, 1892–1950. The title of the
poem is *God's World*.

O my deir hert, young Jesus sweit,
Prepare thy creddil in my spreit,
And I sall rock thee in my hert
And never mair from thee depart.

But·I sall praise thee evermoir
With sangis sweit unto thy gloir;
The knees of my hert sall I bow,
And sing that richt Balulalow.

THE WEDDERBURNS

James, John and Robert Wedderburn were Scottish
poets and religious reformers, 16th century.

The shepherds sing; and shall I silent be?
My God, no hymns for Thee?
My soul's a shepherd too; a flock it feeds
Of thoughts, and words, and deeds;
The pasture is thy word; the streams, thy grace
Enriching all the place.
Shepherd and flock shall sing, and all my powers
Out-sing the day-light houres . . .

GEORGE HERBERT

I got me flowers to strew thy way,
    I got me boughs off many a tree:
But thou wast up by break of day,
    And brought'st thy sweets along with thee . . .

Yet though my flowers be lost, they say
    A heart can never come too late.
Teach it to sing thy praise this day,
    And then this day my life shall date.

GEORGE HERBERT

Pleasure it is
    To hear, iwis,
    The birdès sing.
The deer in the dale,
The sheep in the vale,
    The corn springing;
God's purveyance
For sustenance
    It is for man.
Then we will always
To Him give praise,
    And thank Him than,
    And thank Him than.

WILLIAM CORNYSHE · DIED C. 1523

William Cornyshe, poet, playwright, actor, composer
and favourite of Henry VIII, was in charge of music on
several state occasions.

Almighty One, in the woods I am blessed. Happy everyone
in the woods. Every tree speaks through thee. O God! What
glory in the woodland! On the heights is peace—peace to
serve Him.

BEETHOVEN

You are to me, O Lord,
What wings are to the flying bird.

A DISCIPLE OF RAMAKRISHNA

I pray for a gift which perhaps would be miraculous: simply to be able to see that field of waving grass as I should see it if association and the "film of custom" did not obscure it.

MARK RUTHERFORD

§ 3

We worship and adore the framer and former of the universe; governor, disposer, keeper; Him on whom all things depend; mind and spirit of the world; from whom all things spring; by whose spirit we live; the divine spirit diffused through all; God all-powerful; God always present; God above all other gods; Thee we worship and adore!

SENECA · 4 B.C.–65 A.D. · ROMAN STOIC

Most glorious of immortals, O Zeus of many names, almighty and everlasting, sovereign of nature, directing all in accordance with law, thee it is fitting that all mortals should address . . . Thee all this universe, as it rolls circling round the earth, obeys wheresoever thou dost guide, and gladly owns thy sway . . .

No work upon earth is wrought apart from thee, Lord, nor through the heavenly sphere, nor upon the sea; save only whatsoever wicked deeds men do in their own foolishness. Nay, thou knowest how to make even the rough smooth, and to bring order out of disorder: and things not friendly are friendly in thy sight. For so hast thou fitted all things together, the good with the evil, that there might be one eternal law over all . . . Deliver men from fell ignorance. Banish it, father, from their soul, and grant them to obtain wisdom, whereon relying thou rulest all things with justice.

CLEANTHES · BORN C. 301 B.C. · GREEK STOIC

For to be greatly strong is thine at all times; and the might of thine arm who shall withstand? because the whole world before thee is as a grain in a balance, and as a drop of dew that at the morning cometh down upon the earth. But thou hast mercy on all men, because thou hast power to do all things, and thou overlookest the sins of men to the end they may repent. For thou lovest all things that are, and abhorrest none of the things which thou didst make; for never wouldest thou have formed anything if thou didst hate it. And how would anything have endured, except thou hadst willed it? Or that which was not called by thee, how would it have been preserved? But thou sparest all things, because they are thine, O Sovereign Lord, thou lover of men's lives;

For thine incorruptible spirit is in all things.

THE WISDOM OF SOLOMON

O God, I never hearken to the voices of the beasts or the rustle of the trees, the splashing of waters or the song of birds, the whistling of the wind or the rumble of thunder, but I sense in them a testimony to Thy Unity and a proof of Thy Incomparableness; that Thou art the All-prevailing, the All-knowing, the All-wise, the All-just, the All-true, and that in Thee is neither overthrow nor ignorance nor folly nor injustice nor lying. O God, I acknowledge Thee in the proof of Thy handiwork and the evidence of Thy acts: grant me, O God, to seek Thy Satisfaction with my satisfaction, and the Delight of a Father in His child, remembering Thee in my love for Thee, with serene tranquillity and firm resolve.

DHU 'L-NUN · DIED 861 · SUFI

§ 4

O Sacred Providence, who from end to end
Strongly and sweetly movest! shall I write,
And not of thee, through whom my fingers bend
To hold my quill? shall they not do thee right?

Of all the creatures both in sea and land
Onely to Man thou hast made known thy wayes,
And put the penne alone into his hand,
And made him Secretarie of thy praise. . . .

All things that are, though they have sev'rall wayes,
Yet in their being joyn with one advise
To honour thee: and so I give thee praise
In all my other hymns, but in this twice.

GEORGE HERBERT

My God, I heard this day,
That none doth build a stately habitation,
   But he that means to dwell therein.
   What house more stately hath there been,
Or can be, than is Man? to whose creation
      All things are in decay . . .

For us the windes do blow,
The earth doth rest, heav'n move, and fountains flow.
   Nothing we see, but means our good,
   As our delight, or as our treasure:
The whole is, either our cupboard of food,
      Or cabinet of pleasure.

The starres have us to bed;
Night draws the curtain, which the sunne withdraws·
Musick and light attend our head.
All things unto our flesh are kinde
In their descent and being; to our minde
In their ascent and cause . . .

Since then, my God, thou hast
So brave a Palace built; O dwell in it,
That it may dwell with thee at last!
Till then, afford us so much wit;
That, as the world serves us, we may serve thee,
And both thy servants be.

GEORGE HERBERT

I will praise thee; for I am fearfully and wonderfully
made: marvellous are thy works; and that my soul knoweth
right well.

FROM PSALM 139

If I ascend up into heaven, thou art there: if I make my
bed in hell, behold, thou art there.
If I take the wings of the morning, and dwell in the utter-
most parts of the sea,
Even there shall thy hand lead me, and thy right hand shall
hold me.

FROM PSALM 139

O Adorable and Eternal God! Hast Thou made me a
free agent? And enabled me if I please to offend Thee
infinitely? What other end couldst Thou intend by this, but
that I might please Thee infinitely? That having the power
of pleasing or displeasing, I might be the friend of God! Of

all exaltations in all worlds this is the greatest. To make a world for me was much, to command Angels and men to love me was much, to prepare eternal joys for me was more. But to give me a power to displease Thee, or to set a sin before Thy face, which Thou infinitely hatest, to profane Eternity, or to defile Thy works, is more stupendous than all these. What other couldst Thou intend by it but that I might infinitely please Thee? And having the power of pleasing or displeasing, might please Thee and myself infinitely, in being pleasing! Hereby Thou hast prepared a new fountain and torrent of joys greater than all that went before, seated us in the Throne of God, made us Thy companions, endued us with a power most dreadful to ourselves, that we might live in sublime and incomprehensible blessedness for evermore. For the satisfaction of our goodness is the most sovereign delight of which we are capable. And that by our own actions we should be well pleasing to Thee, is the greatest Felicity Nature can contain. O Thou who art infinitely delightful to the sons of men, make me, and the sons of men, infinitely delightful unto Thee. Replenish our actions with amiableness and beauty, that they may be answerable to Thine, and like unto Thine in sweetness and value. That as Thou in all Thy works art pleasing to us, we in all our works may be so to Thee; our own actions as they are pleasing to Thee being an offspring of pleasures sweeter than all.

THOMAS TRAHERNE

Lord, Thou hast given me my being of such a nature that it can continually make itself more able to receive thy grace and goodness. And this power, which I have of Thee, wherein I have a living image of Thine almighty power, is free will. By this I can either enlarge or restrict my capacity for Thy grace.

NICOLAS OF CUSA

Though our mouths were full of song as the sea, and our tongues of exultation as the multitude of its waves, and our lips of praise as the wide-extended firmament; though our eyes shone with light like the sun and the moon, and our hands were spread forth like the eagles of heaven, and our feet were swift as hinds, we should still be unable to thank thee and to bless thy name, O Lord our God and God of our fathers, for one thousandth or one ten-thousandth part of the bounties which thou hast bestowed upon our fathers and upon us.

THE HEBREW MORNING SERVICE

O my God, my whole life has been a course of mercies and blessings, shown to one who has been most unworthy of them. Year after year Thou hast carried me on, removed dangers from my path, refreshed me, borne with me, directed me, sustained me. O forsake me not, when my strength faileth me. And Thou wilt never forsake me. I may securely repose upon Thee. While I am true to Thee, Thou wilt still, and to the end, be superabundantly good to me. I may rest upon Thy arm; I may go to sleep in Thy bosom. Only give me, and increase in me, that true loyalty to Thee, which is the bond of the covenant between Thee and me, and the pledge in my own heart and conscience that Thou, the Supreme God, wilt not forsake me. Amen.

CARDINAL NEWMAN · 1801-90

Thou art my God, sole object of my love:
Not for the hope of endless joys above;
Not for the fear of endless pains below,
Which they who love thee not must undergo.

For me, and such as me, thou deign'st to bear
An ignominious cross, the nails, the spear:
A thorny crown transpierced thy sacred brow,
While bloody sweats from every member flow.
For me in tortures thou resign'st thy breath,
Embraced me on the cross, and saved me by thy death.
And can these sufferings fail my heart to move?
What but thyself can now deserve my love?
Such as then was, and is, thy love to me,
Such is, and shall be still, my love to thee—
To thee Redeemer! mercy's sacred spring!
My God, my Father, Maker and my King!

UNTRACED

Wheresoever I go, Thou art my companion;
Thou takest me by the hand and guidest me.
As I walk along I lean on Thee,
And thou goest with me carrying my burden.
If in my distress I speak frantically,
Thou commandest my words, and thus
Takest away my shame, and I am made bold.
Now I know that every man is a friend dear to me.
I pray, says Tura, with childish delight;
For I feel Thy bliss within and without me.

TUKARAM

Alone with none but Thee, my God,
    I journey on my way;
What need I fear when Thou art near,
    Oh King of night and day?
More safe am I within Thy hand
    Than if a host did round me stand.

ATTRIBUTED TO ST. COLUMBA · 521–597

How could the Love between Thee and me sever?
As the leaf of the lotus abides on the water: so thou art my
    Lord, and I am Thy servant.
As the night-bird Chakor gazeth all night at the moon: so
    Thou art my Lord and I am Thy servant.
From the beginning until the ending of time, there is love
    between Thee and me; and how shall such love be ex-
    tinguished?
Kabir says: "As the river enters into the ocean, so my heart
    touches Thee."

KABIR

The translation is by Tagore.

Two ways I love Thee: selfishly,
And next, as worthy is of Thee.
'Tis selfish love that I do naught
Save think on Thee with every thought.
'Tis purest love when Thou dost raise
The veil to my adoring gaze.
Not mine the praise in that or this:
Thine is the praise in both, I wis.

RABI'A

Not with doubting, but with assured consciousness do I
love Thee, O Lord. Thou didst strike my heart with Thy
word and I loved Thee. And the heavens too, and the earth
and all therein, manifestly on every side, they bid me love
Thee; nor cease they to say so unto all, that there may be no
excuse . . .
But what do I love when I love Thee? not grace of bodies,
nor the beauty of the seasons, nor the brightness of the
light, so gladsome to these eyes; nor inexhaustible melodies
of sweet song, nor the fragrant smell of flowers, of ointments
and spices, not manna and honey, not limbs acceptable to

embracements of the flesh. None of these love I when I love my God: and yet I love a kind of light, and of melody and of fragrance, a kind of food and a manner of embracement, when I love my God; the embracement, food, fragrance, melody, and light of my inner man; where there shineth unto my soul what space containeth not, and there soundeth what time snatcheth not, and there smelleth what breath disperseth not, and there tasteth what eating cloyeth not, and there clingeth what satiety divorceth not. This is which I love when I love my God.

ST. AUGUSTINE

§ 6

> Dieu d' Abraham, Dieu d' Isaac, Dieu de Jacob,
> Non des philosphes et des savants.
> Certitude. Certitude. Sentiment. Joie. Paix.

This is from the Memorial, or Amulet, of Pascal, a scrap of parchment on which he recorded, in stammering ecstasy, his sudden turning from scholarship to love. It may be translated "God of Abraham, God of Isaac, God of Jacob, not the God of philosophers and scholars. Certainty. Certainty. The heart! Joy. Peace."

Holy, Holy, Holy.

O Thou.

[Let all the earth keep silence before him.]

THE END

Let the words of my mouth, and the meditation of my heart, be acceptable in thy sight, O Lord, my strength and my redeemer.

*

The wolf also shall dwell with the lamb, and the leopard shall lie down with the kid; and the calf and the young lion and the fatling together; and a little child shall lead them.

And the cow and the bear shall feed; their young ones shall lie down together: and the lion shall eat straw like the ox.

And the sucking child shall play on the hole of the asp, and the weaned child shall put his hand on the cockatrice' den.

They shall not hurt nor destroy in all my holy mountain: for the earth shall be full of the knowledge of the Lord, as the waters cover the sea.

A NOTE ABOUT FLOWERS

We have printed no prayers for flowers, because we know none. The following may serve as a substitute.

For the flowers are great blessings,
For the Lord made a Nosegay in the medow with his disciples
  and preached upon the lily.
For the angels of God took it out of his hand and carried it
  to the Height . . .
For there is no Height in which there are not flowers.
For flowers have great virtues for all the senses.
For the flower glorifies God and the root parries the adversary.
For the flowers have their angels even the words of God's
  Creation.
For the warp and woof of flowers are worked by perpetual
  moving spirits.
For flowers are good both for the living and the dead.
For there is a language of flowers.
For there is a sound reasoning upon all flowers.
For elegant phrases are nothing but flowers.
For flowers are peculiarly the poetry of Christ.
For flowers are medicinal.
For flowers are musical in ocular harmony.
For the right names of flowers are yet in heaven, God make
  gardeners better nomenclators.
For the Poorman's nosegay is an introduction to a Prince . . .

CHRISTOPHER SMART

St. Francis ordered a plot to be set aside for the cultiva-
tion of flowers when the convent garden was made, in order
that all who saw them might remember the Eternal Sweetness.

THOMAS OF CELANO

Thomas of Celano was a follower of St. Francis (whom
he joined probably about 1214) and his biographer.

And a note on trees:

Each bush and oak doth know I AM
HENRY VAUGHAN

O never harm the dreaming world,
the world of green, the world of leaves,
but let its million palms unfold
the adoration of the trees . . .
KATHLEEN RAINE · CONTEMPORARY

The tree which moves some to tears of joy is in the eyes
of others only a green thing which stands in the way.
BLAKE

ADDENDUM:

OF GOD AND PRAYER

§ 1

God is the Eternal One, he is everlasting and is without end. He is everlasting and eternal. He endureth for time without end, and he will exist to all eternity.

OLD EGYPTIAN

There is but one God, whose name is true, the Creator, devoid of fear and enmity, immortal, unborn, self-existent, great and bountiful.

THE JAPJI

God is the light of all lights and luminous beyond all the darkness of our ignorance. He is knowledge and the object of knowledge.

THE BHAGAVAD-GITA

In every place where you find the imprint of men's feet there am I.

THE TALMUD

*   *   *

God is seated in the hearts of all.

THE BHAGAVAD-GITA

God is in thy heart, yet thou searchest for him in the wilderness.

THE GRANTH

See note on page 284.

We are enclosed in the Father, and we are enclosed in the Son, and we are enclosed in the Holy Ghost. And the Father is enclosed in us, and the Son is enclosed in us, and the Holy Ghost is enclosed in us: Almightiness, All Wisdom, All Goodness: one God, one Lord.

JULIANA OF NORWICH

I believe that God is in me as the sun is in the colour and fragrance of a flower—the Light in my darkness, the Voice in my silence.

HELEN KELLER

She became blind and deaf in infancy, and did not know there was such a thing as human speech.

Good is holy silence and a giving of holiday to every sense.

EGYPTIAN · 350 B.C.

God wants the heart.

THE TALMUD

§ 2

Prayer is the effort to live in the spirit of the whole.

COLERIDGE

Prayer is
The world in tune.

HENRY VAUGHAN

Prayer is no other but the revelation of the will or mind of God.

JOHN SALTMARSH

He was chaplain in Sir Thomas Fairfax's army.

The people think that they pray before God. But it is not so. For the prayer itself is the essence of the Godhead.

RABBI PINHAS OF KOREZ · HASID

When one says to the great Thinker: "Here is one of thy thoughts: I am thinking it now", that is a prayer—a word to the big heart from one of its own little hearts.

GEORGE MACDONALD

One night a certain man cried "Allah!" till his lips grew
    sweet with praising Him.
The Devil said, "O man of many words, where is the response
    'Here am I' to all this 'Allah'?
Not a single response is coming from the Throne: how long
    will you say 'Allah' with grim face?"
He was broken-hearted and lay down to sleep: in a dream he
    saw Khadir amidst the verdure,
Who said, "Hark, you have held back from praising God:
    why do you repent of calling unto Him?"
He answered. "No 'Here am I' is coming to me in response:
    I fear that I am turned away from the Door."

Said Khadir, "Nay; God saith: That 'Allah' of thine is My
  'Here am I', and that supplication and grief
And ardour of thine is My messenger to thee. Thy fear and
  love are the noose to catch My Favour:
Beneath every 'O Lord' of thine is many a 'Here am I' from
  Me."

JALALU D-DIN RUMI

He it is that desireth in thee, and He it is that is desired.

WALTER HYLTON · DIED. ?1396

It is good if man can bring about that God sings within him.

RABBI ELIMELEKH OF LIZHENSK · HASID

*   *   *

Do never pray,
But only say
—O Thou!

JAMES STEPHENS

Pray only for the suppression of evil, and never for one's
material well-being, for a separating veil arises if one admits
the material into the spiritual.

THE BAAL-SHEM · HASID

See note on page 281.

Some pray: *Let me sleep with that woman!* Do thou,
Marcus, pray: *Let me not lust to sleep with her!* Others pray:
Let me be done with that man! Thou: *Let me not wish to be
done with him!* Others: *Let me not lose my little child!* Thou:

Let me not fear to lose him! In short, pray in this spirit, and await the outcome.

MARCUS AURELIUS

When you pray, endeavour to pray more for others than for yourself alone. . . . Pray for all as you would pray for yourself, with the same sincerity and fervour; look upon their infirmities and sicknesses as your own, their sins and passions as your own, their temptations, misfortunes, and manifold afflictions as your own. Such prayer will be accepted with great favour by the Heavenly Father, the most gracious, common Father of all, that boundless Love which embraces all creatures, that most Holy Spirit who loves the soul that cares for the salvation of others, because He Himself wishes to save us all in every possible way, if only we do not harden our hearts.

JOHN OF CRONSTADT (SHORTENED)

The prayer of one pure heart, I think, hath might
To atone for many.

SOPHOCLES

*　　　*　　　*

I seemed alone with immensity, and there came at last that melting of the divine darkness into the life within me for which I prayed.

A.E. (GEORGE RUSSELL) · 1867–1935

When I prayed in my heart, everything about me appeared to be pleasing and lovely. It was as though the trees, the grass, the birds, the earth, the air and the light were saying that everything prayed, and praised God.

"THE PILGRIM"

The Pilgrim is the unknown author of *The Candid Narrations of a Pilgrim to His Spiritual Father*, first printed in Kazan in 1884. The passage has been shortened.

I am trying to recall, as I write this, what I meant in my young boyhood by praying. I think I meant a process in which getting outside oneself, getting inside oneself, communing with God (very vaguely felt as something all-pervading and good), communing with the leaves and the sky and London and the dahlias in the market gardens, flinging up one's arms and expressing gratitude for the joy of living as one sniffed the air, and making up one's mind to be a better boy so that one shouldn't feel shut out from all these cleannesses and beauties—I think I meant a process in which things of this kind and others like them were somehow all mixed up.

V.G. · FROM *MY DEAR TIMOTHY*

I was utterly alone with the sun and the earth. Lying down on the grass, I spoke in my soul to the earth, the sun, the air, and the distant sea far beyond sight. I thought of the earth's firmness—I felt it bear me up; through the grassy couch there came an influence as if I could feel the great earth speaking to me. I thought of the wandering air—its pureness, which is its beauty; the air touched me and gave me something of itself. I spoke to the sea: though so far, in my mind I saw it, green at the rim of the earth and blue in deeper ocean. . . . I turned to the blue heaven over, gazing into its depth, inhaling its exquisite colour and sweetness. The rich blue of the unattainable flower of the sky drew my soul towards it, and there it rested, for pure colour is rest of heart. By all these I prayed. . . . Then, returning, I prayed by the sweet thyme, whose little flowers I touched with my hand; by the slender grass; by the crumble of dry chalky earth I took up

nd let fall through my fingers. Touching the crumble of
arth, the blade of grass, the thyme flower, breathing the
arth-encircling air, thinking of the sea and the sky, holding
ut my hand for the sunbeams to touch it, prone on the
ward in token of deep reverence, thus I prayed . . .

RICHARD JEFFERIES · 1848–87

* * *

Prayer is the greatest of spells, the best healing of all
emedies.

THE YASHT

The prayer of the heart is the source of all good, which
efreshes the soul as if it were a garden.

ST. GREGORY OF SINAI · DIED 1360

Prayer renews the sixth day of creation.

RABBI MOSHE HAKOTUN

NOTES

I. ON RELIGIONS

HASIDISM

Hasid is a Hebrew word meaning "pious" or "devout", and there were Hasidim in Biblical times. The word and its derivatives are used in this book, however, with exclusive reference to the remarkable Jewish movement which originated in Podolia just before the middle of the eighteenth century and soon had millions of adherents, particularly in Eastern Europe. Martin Buber is its greatest contemporary interpreter. Louis I. Newman has well described the movement as follows: "Its chief emphasis has been upon a sense of mystical ecstasy in the communion of God and man; upon the joyful affirmation of life; upon compassion, charity and love; upon democracy and brotherhood between rich and poor; and upon the moral values of the religious system." He might have added that the Hasidim are exceptional, if not unique, among religious teachers for their use of paradox, their dry humour, and the everyday familiarity of their intercourse with God.

The movement was inspired by the Baalshem (Rabbi Israel b. Eliezer), one of the world's greatest religious geniuses, who lived from 1700 to 1760. He was called the Baalshem ("Master of the Name"), because he could reputedly pronounce the Tetragrammaton, the ineffable name of God.

HINDUISM

(1) Central to Brahmanical Hinduism, for all its polytheistic proliferations, is the conception of an absolute, all-embracing spirit, the Brahma (neuter), the one and only reality, itself unconditioned, and the original cause and ultimate goal of all individual souls. The ceaseless working of the Absolute Spirit as a creative, conservative and destructive principle is represented by the divine Triad of Brahma (masculine), Vishnu and Siva.

The Vedic literature, which goes back to about 1500 B.C., forms the foundation of this system of belief. (Veda means "knowledge", i.e., sacred knowledge.) There are four Vedas, each being a collection of devotional texts: the first of these Vedas is the Rig-veda. Attached to the Vedas are the Upanishads, of a more mystical nature, and tending to pantheistic monism. A passage in one of the Upanishads, for instance, begins with the question "How many Gods are there, O Yajnavolkya?": the first reply is "three and three hundred, three and three thousand", but this is gradually amended to "really" one and a half, and then to one.

(2) Varuna, to whom the beautiful prayer on page 20 is addressed, is the most spiritual and ethical of Vedic deities—"the king of the gods and the universe; the nightly star-spangled firmament".

(3) The Bhagavad-Gita, though in its present form it cannot be earlier than the first or second century A.D., may go back to the fourth century B.C. The central figure is Krishna, who appears as an incarnation of the Deity. "Like the Vision of Isaiah and the Psalms of David," write Swami Prabhavananda and Christopher Isherwood in the preface to their translation of this glorious epic, "it contains ecstatic mystical utterances about the nature and attributes of God . . . Its essential message is timeless. In words which belong to no one language, race or epoch, incarnate God speaks to man, His friend." This "Song of God", it may be added, is one of the sanest guides to practical morality in the world's literature.

(4) Dadu was the founder, about 1600 A.D., of a sect in western India called the Dadu Panthis. Their only form of religious worship is to repeat the name of Rama, whose cult is founded on family life, on fraternal helpfulness, and on humble devotion to a loving Parent, who desires the good of mankind.

(5) Tulsi Das (A.D. 1532–1623) was the greatest of Hindi poets: he renounced the world and entered upon an ascetic life, much of which was spent in preaching the necessity of

a loving faith in Rama. His most famous poem, "The Lake of Rama's Deeds", is said to be better known among Hindus in upper India than the Bible among the English rural population.

MANI

Mani, who lived in Persia in the third century after Christ, was the founder of Manichaeism, a religion widely accepted in Persia, Mesopotamia, Transoxiana and the Roman Empire from the third to the fifth centuries. The basis of the system is the co-existence of a Kingdom of Light (with God as its head) and a Kingdom of Darkness (source of Satan). It is man's duty, by moral living, to free light from darkness: Manichaeans, for instance, were forbidden to kill any living thing. Mani regarded himself as the last and greatest of the prophets, successor to Jesus, "Ambassador of Light": and claimed that only through the instrumentality of himself and his followers could the separation of light from darkness be completed.

MARDUK

Originally, under another name, a mere local god, by the time of Nebuchadnezzar Marduk was tending to become, for the Babylonian priesthood, the God of monotheism: he is indeed usually called "Lord" by Greek and Roman writers.

There is documentary evidence that Nebuchadnezzar was a man of deep religious feeling.

NEOPLATONISM

Originating in Alexandria, and with Plotinus as by far its greatest name, Neoplatonism was the last school of Greek philosophy. "The influence of Neoplatonism on the history of our ethical culture," it has been well said, "is immeasurable, because it begot the consciousness that the only blessedness which can satisfy the heart must be sought higher even than the sphere of reason. That man shall not live by bread alone, the world had learned before Neoplatonism: but Neoplatonism enforced the deeper truth—a truth which the older philosophy had missed—that man shall not live by knowledge alone."

It was from Neoplatonism, above all, that the beautiful flower of Christian mysticism blossomed: and St. Augustine was strongly influenced by it.

Simplicius was one of the last of the Neoplatonists.

SHINTOISM

Shintoism, "The Way of the Gods", is the ancestral religion of Japan. Originating in nature-worship (its deities were gods and goddesses of the sky, earth, sun, moon; of trees, plants, mountains, rivers, sea; of fertility and growth), it was to a great extent, over a long period of its history, a mere instrument of national consolidation. But from the ninth century A.D. to the imperial restoration of 1868 it was greatly influenced by Buddhism, and acquired features of high ethical value.

SIKHISM

The Sikhs originated in the Punjab as a sect of dissenters from Brahmanical Hinduism. Already about A.D. 1100 Jaidev had taught that Yoga was worthless in comparison with the worship of God in thought, word and deed. Later the poet and mystic, Kabir, denounced idolatry and ritualism. The true founder of the sect was, however, Nanak, born in 1469. He was sternly monotheistic, and taught that religious vestments, ostentatious penance, etcetera, were worthless. All men had a right to search for knowledge of God irrespective of caste. His successor in the Guruship (or spiritual leadership) was Guru Angad, who began the compilation of the

Granth Sahib (holy book), in which he included what he had learned from Nanak, adding devotional reflections of his own. At the end of the sixteenth century Arjan became Guru: he enlarged the *Granth*, half of which is his work. A hundred years later Guru Govind Singh made the Sikh initiation a rite of admittance into a militant order; he declared that the line of Gurus was extinct and the Guruship vested in the *Granth* itself. Sikhism was thenceforth to be a militant theocracy.

The Japji is a sort of epitome of Sikh doctrine.

STOICISM

This grave and noble philosophy arose in Athens at the end of the fourth century B.C., drew many of the best Romans to it as a religion to live by, and rapidly lost influence in the third century A.D. It bequeathed a beautiful heritage to Christianity.

Four Stoics are represented in this volume, two Roman and two Greek. The thought of one of the Greeks, the poor, lame and ailing Epictetus, indicates perhaps most clearly what Stoicism meant to its adherents. The summary is from the *Encyclopaedia Britannica*:

God, whose thought directs the universe, has given us, as a good king and father, a will which cannot be compelled or thwarted by anything external. Man is a member of a great system which comprises God and men. Every human being is a citizen of his own commonwealth; but he is also a member of the great city of gods and men, of which the political city is a mere copy. All men are the sons of God by virtue of rationality, and are kindred in nature with him: so they can learn the will of God, which is the will of nature. The natural instinct of animated life, to which man also is subject, is self-preservation and self-interest: but men are so constituted that the individual cannot secure his own interests unless he contributes to the common welfare. Our aim should therefore be to see the world as a whole, to grow into the mind of God and to make the will of nature our own.

(In my day Jews at Oxford studied Epictetus for their Divinity examination, instead of the New Testament.)

Epictetus is closely followed, though perhaps rather less theistically, by the Roman Emperor Marcus Aurelius, whose *Meditations* (called by him "Words addressed to himself") is the best of all bedside books.

SUFISM

Sufism, which arose in the eighth century A.D., was the mysticism of Islam. Mysticism, like God, is one; and though within every mysticism there is a difference of emphasis as between one mystic and another, Islamic mysticism in general shows all the familiar characteristics of, for instance, Christian and Jewish mysticism. (Note especially the extraordinary parallelism of a prayer by Rabi'a, the woman Sufi, and one by a Hasidic Rabbi a thousand years later.) The Sufi poets of Persia, however, exceeded most other mystics in the abandon with which they described the union of God and the soul in terms of earthly love: the greatest of them was Jalalu D-Din Rumi.

ZOROASTER

Zoroaster was the founder of what was the national religion of the Iranian people from the Achaemenian dynasty (558–339 B.C.) to Sassanian times (A.D. 235–651). His dates are unknown; some authorities put him as early as 1000 B.C.

"In the beginning", according to Zoroastrianism, there were two spirits, Ahura, spirit of good, light, life, and Ahriman, spirit of evil, darkness, death. They come into conflict: they create: they struggle for the soul of man, which had been brought into being by Ahura, but endowed by him with free will, and therefore open to the promptings of Ahriman. The fundamental demand of Zoroastrianism is that man, by deed, word and thought, should give Ahura, in "the last days", the final victory.

The Zend-Avesta is the Zoroastrian bible and prayer-book. Its contents include the Yasna (a liturgical book) and the Yashts, or "songs of praise"—but certain Yashts are to be found in the Yasna.

Zoroastrianism is practically extinct in Persia, but Parsees in and around Bombay profess it. In fact, however, they are pure monotheists.

I am indebted to the *Encyclopaedia Britannica* for some of the information in the above notes.

II. OTHER NOTES

THE GAELIC POEMS

All the Gaelic poems in this book are taken from *The Sun Dances: Prayers and Blessings from the Gaelic*, collected and translated by Alexander Carmichael, chosen and with an introduction by Adam Bittleston, and published by the Christian Community Press of 34 Glenilla Road, London, N.W.3, and Edinburgh. We wish to thank the Press for the special generosity with which they have granted our request to print eleven poems: and we urge everyone to buy this quite lovely book. We also thank Sir Hugh Watson, D.K.S., and Mr. A. M. Watson, the Trustees acting under the will of the late Professor James Carmichael Watson, Dr. Alexander Carmichael's grandson.

The Sun Dances is itself an abbreviation of the great five-volume work (to be completed by a sixth volume), entitled *Carmina Gadelica* and published by Oliver and Boyd of Edinburgh, which preserves Dr. Carmichael's life-work.

Dr. Carmichael was born in 1832, and became a civil servant: but his main interest was in the recording of Gaelic poetry and customs. He wrote down, and brilliantly translated, what was recited to him by "men and women throughout the Highlands and Islands of Scotland, from Arran to Caithness, from Perth to St. Kilda": by crofters, cottars, shepherds, lightkeepers and the rest. "It is the product," Dr. Carmichael wrote of his collection, "of far-away thinking come down on the long stream of time. Who the thinkers and whence the stream, who can tell? Some of the hymns may have been composed within the cloistered walls of Derry and Iona and some of the incantations among the cromlechs of Stonehenge and the standing stones of Callarnis. These poems were composed by the learned, but they have not come down through the learned, but through the unlearned." Dr. Kenneth MacLeod records that "one evening a venerable Islesman, carried out of himself for the time being, allowed Dr. Carmichael to take down from him a singularly beautiful 'going into sleep' rune; early next morning the reciter travelled twenty-six miles to exact a pledge that his 'little prayer' should never be allowed to appear in print. 'Think ye,' said the old man, 'if I slept a wink last night for thinking of what I had given away. Proud indeed shall I be if it gives pleasure to yourself, but I should not like all eyes to read it in a book.' In the writer's presence the manuscript was handed over to the reciter to be burnt there and then".

ARCHBISHOP LAUD'S PRAYER AND THE KNIGHTS' PRAYER

We are in some difficulty about both these prayers. Barbara Greene wrote them down many years ago, with the attributions we have given them: but she has lost her copies and we have failed to trace the originals. There is a prayer very similar to the one we have attributed to Laud in Volume

III (page 53) of his Works (Oxford, 1853), several of the phrases being identical: but it is shorter, and differs, though not essentially, in one or two other respects. As to "The Knights' Prayer", Barbara Greene remembers clearly that it was described, in the document from which she copied it, as being in use, at some period, by an Order of Knighthood.

"THE HYMN OF JESUS"

Evelyn Underhill, following G. R. S. Mead, regards this beautiful poem as a dramatic dialogue, in which "the Logos, or Eternal Christ, is represented as matching with His own transcendent, self-giving desire every need of the soul. The soul says 'I would be saved' and Christ replies 'And I would save' [and so on]".

ACKNOWLEDGMENTS

As is explained in the preface, those of the prayers that have been collected by Barbara Greene were jotted down over a period of many years, with no thought of publication. In some cases she failed to make a note of the source. While, therefore, we have done our utmost to trace copyright translations and obtain the necessary permission, we may unwittingly have appropriated the work of others without acknowledgment. We ask pardon for any such transgressions.

*

For the Old and New Testaments the Authorised Version has been used: it is Crown Copyright, and is used by permission. For the (Old Testament) Apocrypha the Revised Version has been used, by permission of the University Presses of Oxford and Cambridge. We have used the Authorised Daily Prayer Book of the United Hebrew Congregations of the British Empire (which was translated by the late Rev. S. Singer), and the extracts are printed by permission of the Singer Prayer Book Publication Committee.

*

The citing of the names of authors, publishers, translators, copyright-holders, etc., below will please be understood as acknowledging kind permission to reprint.

*

THE ACTS OF JOHN. From *The Apocryphal New Testament* tr. by Montague James (Clarendon Press).
A.E. From *The Candle of Vision* (Macmillan).

AL-ANSARI. In part from *Sufism* by A. J. Arberry (Allen and Unwin).

ARJAN. From Macauliffe's *The Sikh Religion* (Clarendon Press).

BELLOC, HILAIRE. From *Sonnets and Verse* (Duckworth).

THE BHAGAVAD-GITA. The passages translated by Swami Prabhavananda and Christopher Isherwood are from the edition published by Phoenix House under the title *The Song of God*.

COLUM, PADRAIC. From *Collected Poems* (Oxford University Press).

DHU 'L-NUN. From *Sufism* by A. J. Arberry (Allen and Unwin).

DRINKWATER, JOHN. From *The Collected Poems of John Drinkwater* (Sidgwick and Jackson).

ELIOT, T. S. From *Murder In The Cathedral* (Faber).

EGYPTIAN PRAYERS. Those translated by Professor J. H. Breasted are quoted in *Religious Life In Ancient Egypt* by Flanders Petrie (Constable).

GASCOYNE, DAVID. From *Poems, 1937-1942* (Mandeville Publications).

GREGORY OF SINAI, ST. Quoted by St. Nilus Sorsky in *A Treasury of Russian Spirituality* ed. by G. P. Fedotor (Sheed and Ward).

HEARD, GERALD. From *Prayers and Meditations*. We thank Mr. Gerald Heard for permission and Harper and Row, New York, for Canadian permission.

HOPKINS, GERARD MANLEY. From *Poems of Gerard Manley Hopkins* (Oxford University Press).

IBN 'ATA' ALLAH OF ALEXANDRIA. From *Sufism* by A. J. Arberry (Allen and Unwin).

IBRAHIM b. ADHAM. In part from *Sufism* by A. J. Arberry (Allen and Unwin).

JALALU D-DIN RUMI. The passage translated by Robert Bridges and Hasan Shahid Suhrawardy is from *The Spirit of Man* by Robert Bridges (Longmans, Green). We thank Miss Elizabeth Daryish. The other passage is from *Rumi: Poet and Mystic* by Reynold A. Nicholson (Allen and Unwin).

JAPJI, THE. From Macauliffe's *The Sikh Religion* (Clarendon Press).

KABIR. From *One Hundred Poems of Kabir* tr. by Tagore (Macmillan). We thank also the Trustees of the Tagore Estate.

MECHTHILD OF MAGDEBURG. From *Das fliessende Licht der Gottheit*, quoted in Evelyn Underhill's *Mysticism* (Methuen), where Margaret Robinson is acknowledged as the translator.

MILLAY, EDNA ST. VINCENT. The poem *God's World* is from *Renascence and Other Poems* and is quoted by permission of Mrs. Norma Millay Ellis.

MIRROR OF PERFECTION, THE. The translation is by Robert Steele (Everyman, Dent).

NICOLAS OF CUSA. From *The Vision of God* tr. by Emma Gurney Salter (Dent).

PÉGUY. From *Basic Verities* tr. by Ann and Julian Green (Routledge and Kegan Paul).

"PILGRIM, THE". From *The Way of a Pilgrim* tr. by Nina Toumanova in *A Treasury of Russian Spirituality* ed. by G. P. Fedotov (Sheed and Ward).

PRUDENTIUS. From *Wandering Scholars* by Helen Waddell (Constable).

RABI'A. One quotation is from *Sufism* by A. J. Arberry (Allen and Unwin).

RAINE, KATHLEEN. From her *Collected Poems*, published by Hamish Hamilton. We thank Miss Raine for kindly relaxing a rule.

RAMAKRISHNA. Probably from *Sri Ramakrishna, Prophet of New India* tr. by Swami Nikhilananda (Harper and Row, New York).

RIG-VEDA. From *Lamps of Fire* by Juan Mascaró (Methuen).

RUTHERFORD, MARK. From *More Pages from a Journal* (Oxford University Press). We thank Mrs. D. V. White.

SINGH, GOVIND. One prayer is from Macauliffe's *The Sikh Religion* (Clarendon Press), and the other from Singh Puran's *The Book of the Ten Masters* (Selwyn and Blount).

SITWELL, EDITH. From *Invocation*. We thank her for a special graciousness. We are also indebted to her for the anonymous evening prayer (page 137), and for the extracts from Christopher Smart, which we have taken from her great anthology *The Atlantic Book of British and American Poetry*.

SOPHOCLES. From the translation of the *Oedipus Coloneus* by Gilbert Murray (Allen and Unwin).

STEPHENS, JAMES. From *Collected Poems*, by permission of Macmillan and Mrs. Iris Wise.

SUSO, HEINRICH. From *The Life of Blessed Henry Suso by Himself* tr. by T. F. Knox (Methuen).

TADHG ÓG Ó HUIGINN. From *A Celtic Miscellany* tr. by Kenneth Hurlstone Jackson (Routledge and Kegan Paul).

TAGORE. Two of the poems are from *Gitanjali*, and the other from *Sadhana*. Published by Macmillan. We thank also the Trustees of the Tagore Estate.

TAHIR. From *The Spirit of Man* by Roger Bridges (Long
mans, Green). We thank Miss Elizabeth Daryish.
TALMUD, THE. From *A Rabbinic Anthology* (Macmillan).
TRAHERNE. From *Centuries of Meditation* (Clarendon Press

UPANISHADS. From Hume's *The Thirteen Principal Upan
shads* (Oxford University Press, Bombay).

VISION OF PIERS PLOWMAN, THE: version by Henry W. Well
(Sheed and Ward).

YASHT, THE. From Muller's *Sacred Books of the East* (Claren
don Press).
YASNA, THE. From Muller's *Sacred Books of the East* (Claren
don Press).

We thank Allenson and Co. Ltd for permission to us
several extracts from *Great Souls at Prayer*.
We thank Lady Gollancz for permission to quote th
version of the Cynewulf hymn by Sir Israel Gollancz.
We thank Messrs. Eulenberg for permission to reproduc
the passage from Beethoven's Quartet in A minor.
Our acknowledgment of permission to quote the Gaeli
poems will be found in the note on page 287.

INDEX

FOR MANUSCRIPT PRAYERS